THE GODODDIN

The Oldest Scottish Poem

THE GODODDIN

The Oldest Scottish Poem

KENNETH HURLSTONE
JACKSON

EDINBURGH *at the University Press*

1969

© K. H. Jackson 1969
EDINBURGH UNIVERSITY PRESS
22 George Square, Edinburgh 8
North America
Aldine Publishing Company
320 West Adams Street, Chicago
Australia and New Zealand
Hodder & Stoughton Ltd
Africa, Oxford University Press
India, P. C. Manaktalu & Sons
Far East, M. Graham Brash & Son
85224 049 x
Library of Congress
Catalog Card Number 68-58881

Printed in Great Britain by
W. & J. Mackay & Co Ltd, Chatham

Contents

Appendix

Part II : The Poems

Preface

The poems discussed in this book have been edited and translated a number of times, notably in Skene's *Four Ancient Books of Wales* (Edinburgh, 1868), I, 374–427, and II, 62–107. But the very early Welsh in which they are composed is so full of obscurities that comparatively little was made of them, beyond the broad outlines, and so-called 'translations' were often absurd – even Sir Edward Anwyl's in the *Transactions of the Honourable Cymmrodorion Society*, 1909–10, pp. 95–136, was by no means wholly satisfactory. In fact, the whole thing was still a riddle until Sir Ifor Williams' epoch-making edition of 1938, *Canu Aneirin* (Cardiff, the University of Wales Press), which put the entire study of the poems of Aneirin on a new and infinitely superior footing.

Comparatively little work has been done, however, in the thirty years since that time, and apart from some matters of detail the interpretation of the text remains what it was in 1938. The time is still not ripe for a full and confident translation, since far too many obscurities remain, and indeed it probably never will be entirely ripe, as it is not likely that many of them ever can be solved. Of one section, the Gorchan of Maeldderw, running to sixty-eight lines, Sir Ifor Williams remarked 'From here on, I can do nothing but make an attempt at an occasional word, . . . and I see nothing but a ray of uncertain light here and there' (*Canu Aneirin* p. 373 f.). Admittedly, the Gorchan of Maeldderw is by far the most difficult piece in the Book of Aneirin, and also Williams was being a good deal too modest. Nevertheless, anyone working on the text as a whole must often echo his words, and it would be quite premature yet to offer what could be called a 'full' translation. What I have tried to do here, in Part ii, is primarily to treat the poems, verse by verse, with tentative 'full' translations, whether of whole verses or only parts of verses, where possible, and otherwise certain passages only – sometimes only summaries; the principles are explained further below in the introductory Note to Part ii.

This book is an *œuvre de vulgarisation*. The chief reason for writing it is that Williams' great work, like almost all his others, was published in Welsh and is consequently quite inaccessible to a very large public outside Wales to which it is – or should be – a matter of the greatest interest. I have in mind two groups of people in particular, in addition to the proverbial 'intelligent general reader'. First, the large and growing body of students of the history and archaeology of Britain in the Dark Ages. Most of these have heard of the *Gododdin* and have a vague idea of what it is about and why it is important for the history of northern Britain about AD 600, but little more than that. Second, there are many whose interests in comparative literature have led them to the study of early heroic poetry, and who have heard of the *Gododdin* as being such a poem but – again – little more than that. The book is in fact an expansion of a lecture given in London University to the 'London Seminar on Epic' in March 1965. Representatives of both the above groups have urged me to publish this material. One would like to add also, third, those who take a general interest in the literature of Britain, and a particular one in the poetry of Scotland.

By contrast, however, it is not intended for Welsh scholars. They will not find here much that is new to them –

apart, perhaps, chiefly from some points given in the Appendix. This is because most of Williams' work is so wholly convincing, and so little has been done on the subject since his time.

Lastly, what is meant by calling the *Gododdin* 'the oldest Scottish poem'? Is it not a Welsh poem? Certainly it exists in a manuscript written in Wales, in the Welsh language, in a Welsh library. At the same time, scholars are nowadays for the most part agreed that it or its nucleus must have been composed in Scotland, very likely in Edinburgh, in the northern dialect of Brittonic spoken in that region and often called 'Cumbric', which, at the date in question, is likely to have differed very little from contemporary Welsh; and if there were such differences, and if we had any means of recognising them, most of them would in any case have disappeared in the process of subsequent transmission for centuries in Wales. It is clear, further, that the heroes commemorated were almost all from Scotland, and there is reason to think that Aneirin, traditionally the author, was so too. As for 'oldest', the date about 600, if correct, naturally puts it centuries before anything generally regarded as a 'Scottish' poem. It is true that there is another – small – group of very early northern British poems in Welsh, about a dozen out of the many attributed to Taliesin, which if genuine would be a little older than the *Gododdin*. But though the kingdom of the prince to whom they are addressed, Urien of Rheged, was – like Gododdin – partly in Scotland and partly in England, its capital seems to have been Carlisle in England whereas that of Gododdin was Edinburgh in Scotland. Besides which the evidence for dating the Taliesin poems so early, though strong *a priori*, is less strong than in the case of the *Gododdin*; and their tradition makes their author a Welshman. So let us agree to call the *Gododdin*, with its linked *gorchanau*, 'the oldest Scottish poem' in the sense here defined.

Abbreviations

AES. A. O. Anderson, *Early Sources of Scottish History A.D. 500–1286* (Edinburgh, 1922)

AS. P. Clemoes and others, *The Anglo-Saxons, Studies Presented to Bruce Dickins* (London, Bowes and Bowes, 1959)

BBCS. *The Bulletin of the Board of Celtic Studies*

BIK. W. Meid (ed.), *Beiträge zur Indogermanistik und Keltologie* (Pokorny festschrift); *Innsbrucker Beiträge zur Kulturwissenschaft*, XIII (Innsbruck, 1967)

CA. Sir Ifor Williams, *Canu Aneirin* (Cardiff, 1938)

CLH. Sir Ifor Williams, *Canu Llywarch Hen* (Cardiff, 1953)

CPNS. W. J. Watson *The History of the Celtic Place-Names of Scotland* (Edinburgh, 1926)

CT. Sir Ifor Williams, *Canu Taliesin* (Cardiff, 1960)

Cymm. *Y Cymmrodor*

Cymm Trans. *The Transactions of the Honourable Society of Cymmrodorion*

EHR. *English Historical Review*

ES. H. M. Chadwick, *Early Scotland*
(Cambridge, 1949)

FT. M. Förster, *Der Flussname Themse;*
Sitzungsberichte der Bayerischen
Akademie der Wissenschaften,
Philosophisch-historische Abteilung,
1941 (Munich, 1942)

G. J. Lloyd-Jones, *Geirfa Barddoniaeth Gynnar*
Gymraeg (Cardiff, 1931–63)

GL. H. M. and N. K. Chadwick, *The Growth*
of Literature, vol. I (Cambridge, 1932)

GPC. *Geiriadur Prifysgol Cymru, A Dictionary of the*
Welsh Language (Cardiff, 1950–)

HW. Sir J. M. Lloyd, *A History of Wales*
(3rd ed., London, Longmans, 1939)

LHEB. Kenneth Jackson, *Language and*
History in Early Britain (Edinburgh, 1953)

OIT. Kenneth Jackson, *The Oldest Irish*
Tradition, a Window on the Iron Age
(Cambridge, 1964)

PP. F. T. Wainwright and others, *The Problem*
of the Picts (Edinburgh, 1955)

RBES. R. G. Collingwood and J. N. L. Myres,
Roman Britain and the English Settlements
(2nd ed., Oxford, 1937)

SEBC. N. K. Chadwick and others, *Studies in the*
Early British Church (Cambridge, 1958)

SEBH. N. K. Chadwick and others, *Studies in*
Early British History (Cambridge, 1954)

TYP. R. Bromwich, *Trioedd Ynys Prydain,*
The Welsh Triads (Cardiff, 1961)

PART I

Introduction

Introduction

The Story

The *Gododdin* poem and three of the four *gorchanau* or separate lays closely associated with it, contained in a thirteenth-century Welsh manuscript now in the Free Library at Cardiff, are attributed to the poet Aneirin who, tradition says, lived in the second half of the sixth century. The *Gododdin* exists in the manuscript in two incomplete and only partly overlapping texts, an archaic one (B.) consisting of forty-two verses, and a less archaic one (A.) of eighty-eight verses, averaging together roughly ten lines per verse in Williams' edition. The four *gorchanau* are respectively sixty-four, fifteen, seventy-five, and sixty-nine lines, but the second, the Gorchan of Adebon, is a freak, as we shall see. These matters are discussed below, but it will be convenient to start here with an account of what the poems tell us about their ostensible historical background, and to see how far this may be a genuine one. We have to bear in mind that the *Gododdin* and its *gorchanau* are not narrative poems but elegies on a number of heroes killed in a battle. Each verse of the *Gododdin* commemorates either some one individual hero (as also do the *gorchanau* except the Gorchan of Adebon), or the army as a whole, praising them and mourning for them; and nowhere is there any attempt to give an account of what it was really all about. Nevertheless it is possible to infer a good deal by way of broad outline, and the following is what we find.

There was a king or chief called Mynyddog, sometimes entitled *Mwynfawr*, 'the Wealthy' or 'the Luxurious'. Both his land and the men of his land, and consequently the poem, are Gododdin,[1] but as a general racial term the men are called Brython. His capital is Eidyn, also called Din Eidyn, 'the Fort of Eidyn'. Mynyddog had gathered together an army of warriors, chiefly his own men from Gododdin itself, but others too from other parts of Britain such as from 'beyond Bannog', from 'beyond the sea of Iuddew', from Aeron, from Elfed, and from Gwynedd including Rhufoniog, Eifionydd, and Mon.

The army is constantly referred to in both texts as consisting of three hundred men, but there is a secondary variant found once in the A. text and once in the Gorchan of Cynfelyn and its rubric to the effect that there were three hundred and sixty-three. Mynyddog feasted this warband for a year in the great hall of Eidyn, perhaps awaiting a favourable moment, and then sent them out to attack the enemy. It is nowhere made clear that he led the expedition himself, which must therefore mean that he did not; and this again must imply, in Dark Age thought, that he was either too old or too ill to do so. The enemy is called Lloegrwys, 'men of Lloegr', and more specifically Dewr (or Deifr) and Brynaich; the terms Saeson and Eingl also occur for them, respectively twice and once, and they are described as *gynt* and *gynhon*, 'heathens', and as a host of a hundred thousand men. The two armies met at a place repeatedly referred to as Catraeth, and the war-band of Mynyddog was annihilated. The version which makes it three hundred men says that only one escaped home alive; while that which has it as three hundred and sixty-three tells that three came back, and also the poet himself

---

[1] NB., *not* Manaw Gododdin; see the Appendix, no. I.

(who would probably count as an extra man, an 'observer' rather than a warrior).

It is fortunate that enough is known about these names and situations to be able to interpret, in terms of the history of Britain in the Dark Ages, what it is that the poem is envisaging. Mynyddog himself is quite unknown, but the identification of Gododdin is generally agreed. It is the country and the tribe which in the preceding, Romano-British, period were known as *Wotādinī*. Our authority for this is the Greek geographer Ptolemy, who in the middle of the second century AD put together a 'Geography' of the known world; his sources for Britain were Roman ones. Welsh *Gododdin* would come quite directly from the older, British, *Wotādinī*.[1] Now according to Ptolemy the country of this tribe reached from the region round the head of the Firth of Forth as far south as the neighbourhood of the Wear in Co. Durham, including all Lothian (though not the upland country of Peeblesshire, Selkirkshire, and Roxburghshire), and therefore Edinburgh. Mynyddog's men are *Brython*, 'Britons', and it should be noted that they are nowhere called *Cymry*, 'Welshmen'; in spite of the fact that this term, meaning literally 'fellow-countrymen' and apparently a product of the post-Roman period of the fifth and sixth centuries, applied equally to the Britons of the north, as may be seen in early Scottish Latin sources which call the men of south-western Scotland *Cumbrenses*, and to the present day in the name Cumberland. *Din Eidyn*, 'the Fort of Eidyn', is Edinburgh itself; it is the truly native, Brittonic, name of the capital, 'translated' by the Anglo-Saxons as *Edin-burh* and by the contemporary Gaelic Scots of the north-west as *Dún Éiden* (modern *Dùn Éideann*), both of which mean exactly the same thing, 'the Fort of Eidyn'.[2] *Bannog* is a range of uplands known elsewhere in

[1] On this name see further the Appendix below, no. 1.

[2] On some questions connected with this name see further the Appendix, no. 2.

Welsh tradition as an important strategic boundary in Scotland. It is the massif which almost entirely blocks the narrow land neck of Scotland between Stirling and Dumbarton, consisting of the Fintry, Kilsyth, Campsie, and Kilpatrick Hills; the Bannock Burn, which takes its name from this range, flows out of the Fintry Hills into the Forth near Stirling.[1] The hero from 'beyond Bannog' came, therefore, from the country of the Picts, which began north of the Forth and of the Bannog hills. *Iuddew*, it is agreed, is the same place as Bede's *Urbs Giudi*, which he associates in a rather obscure sentence, a sentence which has caused some perplexity, with the 'middle' of the Firth of Forth. The name is discussed further in the Appendix, no. 1 below, where it is suggested that Stirling is meant; but however that may be, 'the sea of Iuddew' must surely be the Firth of Forth, and the warrior from 'beyond' it is another Pict, or possibly a Gododdin man from northern Manaw.[2] *Aeron* is generally accepted as being the country round the river *Ayr* in Ayrshire.[3] *Elfed* is the name of a region in and to the east of the Yorkshire Pennines between Aire and Wharfe, including Leeds; it still survives in Barwick-in-Elmet and Sherburn-in-Elmet near Leeds, where *Elmet* represents the form in which the name was borrowed from the Britons by the Anglo-Saxons (the *silva Elmete* of Bede).[4] *Gwynedd* is the modern counties of Anglesey and Caernarvon and parts of those of Merioneth, Denbigh, and Flint; *Rhufoniog* and *Eifionydd* are districts in it, the former in western Denbighshire and the latter roughly between Snowdon and Pwllheli; while *Mon* is Anglesey. It appears, then, that Mynyddog's campaign had been prepared carefully, and that picked warriors had

[1] On Bannog see further the Appendix, no. 3.
[2] On which name see the Appendix, no. 1.
[3] See Cymm. XXVIII, 76 f.; CPNS., p. 342 f.
[4] See A. H. Smith, *The Place-Names of the West Riding of Yorkshire*, IV (English Place-Name Society, XXXIII; Cambridge, 1961), pp. 1 ff.

been called to it, as if to a crusade, not only from Gododdin but also from other parts of British northern Britain and even from North Wales; on the reason for the inclusion of this last see § 8 below.

As for 'the men of Lloegr', this is the ordinary Welsh word for 'England', though its origin and etymology are highly obscure.[1] *Dewr*, or *Deifr*, and *Brynaich* are the two Anglo-Saxon provinces of Deira and Bernicia which became united early in the seventh century into what was known thereafter as Northumbria; Deira being Yorkshire, and Bernicia at first Durham and Northumberland but later including much of southern Scotland.[2] *Saeson* is simply 'the Saxons', coming directly from Latin *Saxones*, and *Eingl* is similarly the Angles, from *Angli*. The English settlers of the north were of course Angles, not Saxons, but the early Welsh used *Saeson* in general of all their Anglo-Saxon enemies, and frequently did not distinguish the Angles from them.[3] The men of Deira and Bernicia were converted to Christianity in the year 627 by the mission of Paulinus from Canterbury, but reverted to heathenism in 632, and were not again converted till Aidan's mission from Iona in 634. As to *Catraeth*, there is every reason to accept the general opinion that this is Catterick in northern Yorkshire (Deira),[4] on the Great North Road about four miles south of Scotch Corner and about ten miles south of the Tees, the boundary between Deira and Bernicia. Catterick was the site of the Romano-British town of Caturactonium (Ptolemy) or Cataracto (Antonine Itinerary), and continued during the Dark Ages as a royal *villa* or 'capital' of the Northumbrian kings. Verse 41 of the A.

[1] An attempt in BBCS. XIX, 8 ff. to derive it from the first element of the name Leicester, and to identify it originally with the Anglo-Saxon kingdom of Middle Anglia, is untenable on philological grounds. See my forthcoming note in BBCS. XXIII, p. 26 f.

[2] For these names see the Appendix, no. 4.

[3] For a suggestion as to the reason for this, see Appendix, no. 5.

[4] For discussion, see the Appendix, no. 6.

text of the *Gododdin* describes the slaughtered army of Mynyddog as 'men cut down in Lloegr', which evidently means that Catraeth was regarded as already within the lands of the English by the time of the battle. On the other hand, the very ancient Taliesin poems addressed to Urien in the latter part of the sixth century speak of him as 'lord of Catraeth', and of 'the men of Catraeth about their prince Urien'; which should mean that in his time Rheged still extended not only right up the Eden valley but also across the Pennines and at least into the fringes of the low country opposite to the east.

§ 2

The Historical Background

It would seem, then, on the face of it, that the poem purports to tell us about the defeat of an attack made by the king of Gododdin in SE Scotland and the NE corner of England, centred in Edinburgh, against the English of Deira and Bernicia, the battle having taken place at Catterick just inside Deira. Does this fit intelligibly into what is known of the history of northern Britain in the Dark Ages, and if so, at what date? The answer is that it does, about the year 600. The English occupation of northern England began in the fifth century with the settlement of the Yorkshire Wolds, spreading over the East Riding in general and linking up with another very early focus round York itself. By the end of the sixth century it is likely that all Yorkshire east of and including the Vale of York was in the hands of the English – it is hardly probable, for one thing, that Catterick would have been a royal *villa*, important enough to have been the scene of the Conversion of Deira in 627, if it was acquired much later than this – and very likely they were already beginning to push into the Pennines. Here, however, expansion was barred, at least in the centre, by the British kingdom of Elfed as long as it lasted, protected by the marshes of the lower Ouse, and it was not conquered until soon after the beginning of the reign of Edwin of Northumbria in 617, who expelled its native king Ceredig. By about 600 the English population of the large parts of Deira which they held is likely to have been fairly considerable as these things go in Dark Age terms.

As for Bernicia, the colony here began, according to Anglo-Saxon tradition, with the occupation of Bamburgh near Lindisfarne by Ida, dated by Bede in the year 547, which is however probably about ten years too early. Everything known about it – and not much is known – suggests that during much of the second half of the sixth century it was a comparatively slight affair, occupying scattered sites along the maritime strip between the Tyne and the Tweed, chiefly in the lower Tyne valley itself and in the coastal regions between Tweed and Aln. Early Welsh 'historical' saga tradition, represented by two separate but complementary sources (Nennius' *Historia Brittonum*, and very early Welsh poetry, some of it perhaps older than the *Gododdin* itself), is definite in telling how various northern British princes, led by the king of Rheged, Urien, and his sons, fought with Ida's successors; and that Urien was betrayed and killed when beseiging the English in Lindisfarne. According to Nennius the Bernician king at that time was Theodric, whose reign is generally dated 572–9 on the basis of the Moore Memoranda, but his account is a little confused and another king, Hussa, may be meant, whose date on the same evidence would be 585–92. But these dates are not reliable, and it is quite probable that Theodric was later than Hussa, and that the killing of Urien is to be put roughly about 590.[1] In 593 Æthelfrith

---

[1] Mr. D. P. Kirby has made a case for dating the reign of Hussa 579–86 and that of Theodric 586–93 (EHR, LXXVIII, 525 f.). See also P. Hunter Blair in SEBH., pp. 149 ff.

became king of Bernicia in succession to Theodric. In 603 Aedán, king of the Scots of the Irish kingdom of Dál Riada in Argyll, led a great army against him to a place called by Bede *Degsastán*, the site of which is unknown.[1] According to the Irish annals he had help from an Irish prince of the powerful northern Uí Néill, and there is some evidence that one of Hussa's sons had joined him as captain of the army. The result was that the Scots were defeated with the loss of all but a few.[2] Almost immediately after this, in 605, Æthelfrith made himself master of Deira, expelling its king Edwin, and fused the two kingdoms into Northumbria, over which he reigned till his death in 617; but there is some reason to think that a Bernician prince called Æthelric had already seized power in Deira about 588 or 590, though he had been succeeded there by a Deiran king Frithuwald by 597 at latest.[3] According to Bede, Æthelfrith conquered more land from the Britons, killing off or subjugating the inhabitants and making them tributary or planting settlers there, than any other king [before him?].[4] He adds that it was in reaction to Æthelfrith's successes that Aedán attacked him at Degsastán. The expansion of the English from the Tweed across the Lammermuirs into Lothian took place during the reign of Edwin, who returned to Northumbria in 617 and was killed in 634, when Northumbria fell apart again, and there is some good reason to think that Edinburgh was captured in 638, in the reign of Oswy king of Bernicia.[5] With this, the kingdom of Gododdin must finally have collapsed.

[1] See Hunter Blair, op. cit. p. 157 n.
[2] *Sed cum paucis victus aufugit*; Bede, 'Historia Ecclesiastica', I, XXXIV.
[3] See Kirby, op. cit. p. 526 f.; and for a new account of the obscure history of Bernicia and Deira at this period, see the whole article, pp. 514 ff.
[4] Loc. cit.
[5] See AS. pp. 35 ff.

§3

The Place of the *Gododdin* in the History of the North

If we ask ourselves how the story of the battle of Catraeth will fit the above picture, it is clear first from what has just been said that it must have taken place before 638. Again, since the English are heathen, some time before 627 is indicated. The presence of a hero from Elfed in Mynyddog's army may well mean it was before that kingdom ceased to exist soon after 617 (though he could have been a later refugee from it). On the other hand, unless Welsh saga greatly misleads us, Urien and his sons were the spearhead of the British resistance to the English in the north a generation or so before this, and if he was still alive it seems hardly likely he would not have joined in this British crusade against them. In his day, he not only fought the English but he succeeded in bottling up their king in Lindisfarne island, as if he had pretty well swept them into the sea, though he was betrayed to his death as a result. This seems to imply that Bernicia was still relatively weak, and that the great expansion of its power under Æthelfrith had not yet begun; indeed it is very plausible that that expansion was made possible by the removal of Urien and the collapse of the alliance of British kings in the north which he had organised. But if Aedán was reacting to Æthelfrith's successes these must have begun with his accession in 593; and certainly after 605, when he acquired Deira, Æthelfrith would have been a most formidable enemy, far too much so to be attacked by the little force that went from Eidyn to Catraeth.[1] Now,

---

[1] According to Kirby, Æthelric's seizure of Deira about 588 or 590 must mean that Bernicia was already sufficiently powerful to be able to make an attack on Deira without endangering its own security (op. cit. p. 527). But the story of Æthelric is by no means very certain, nor are his dates, and it is not impossible that he was not a Bernician at all but a prince of Deira.

Urien's death may have been about 590, or not earlier
than 586 when Theodric quite probably became king.
This seems to give us a date for Catraeth between 586 and
say 605.

To attempt to narrow things any further we must consider what it was that Mynyddog was trying to do. It
seems clear that it was a long-premeditated attack, on
both Bernicia and Deira, and that he had set himself the
same task as Aedán did – to smash the dangerously growing
power of the English on his borders, and indeed well inside
them in the case of Bernicia, before it was too late. Was he
imitating Aedán or vice versa? It is really not possible to
say; but if the story of the three hundred men is true – a
point to be examined in a moment – it must surely be that
Æthelfrith's great expansions, and increase in power, had
not yet seriously begun, and Mynyddog was taking his last
chance, foreseeing that soon it would be too late. At any
rate the poem implies that though the expedition failed,
Mynyddog's action was a long-considered one, and this
suggests that he thought it had a good chance. One would
therefore be inclined to look for an early date rather than
a late one, while Bernicia was still not yet too strong. But
the politics of the Britons, the Bernicians, and the Deirans
are too obscure at this period, with too many unknown
factors, to be able to be more precise; for instance the
significance and reliability of the tale of Æthelric are both
doubtful.

Bearing in mind, however, that the enemy is the men of
Bernicia *and* Deira, and accepting the truth of that tale,
one may perhaps suggest that it well fits the period about
588–90. Æthelric, a prince of Bernicia, is in process of
setting up in Deira, and is thus able to draw on the forces
of both kingdoms in alliance, but has weakened Bernicia
temporarily in consequence. Mynyddog sees his chance
and attacks, before Æthelric shall have had time to con-
solidate his position further. This is of course speculation.

At any rate, the implications of the fact that the enemy is the men of Deira and Bernicia, and that the battle was fought at Catterick, should not be forgotten. It seems to be an allied army rather than a united one, and the point of attacking them at Catterick would surely be the well-known strategic principle of hitting such an alliance at the point of junction, where coherence is weakest. From Edinburgh, Mynyddog had a choice of two routes to Catterick. His troop could either march down the east coast route, along the old Roman road via Carter Bar, High Rochester, Corbridge, and Pierce Bridge on the Tees, or down the other, via Crawford, Carlisle, Penrith, Appleby, and Stanemoor, arriving in either case at Scotch Corner. If they took the former they would expose themselves to the whole line of the Bernician coastal settlements; particularly, at any rate, on reaching the Tyne at Corbridge, though much of the route is across high uplands far from the sea. This would perhaps argue for an early date, while Bernicia was still very weak. By the other route, however, they would be very far away from any English colony, and protected by immense miles of hilly country, all the way until they crossed Stanemoor and came down on Catterick, aiming plumb at the joint between Bernicia and Deira; and it is for this reason that O. G. S. Crawford argued that the latter is more probable.[1] This need not demand a Bernicia so feeble that its men were unable to prevent a long-awaited attack outflanking them along the actual fringes of their entire western border.

§ 4

The Army of Three Hundred

Here arises a further question. Is it credible that an army of three hundred men (or three hundred and sixty-three

[1] *Antiquity*, 1939, pp. 32 ff.

either) could have been sent on such an errand, by anyone in his senses, against two whole kingdoms, whose united army is said by the poet in verse 10 of the A. version to have numbered a hundred thousand; or, more temperately, to have been 180 for every one of the Britons, that is, fifty-four thousand[1] (B. verse 19)? Even allowing for poetic licence here and taking 'a hundred thousand' to mean simply 'a very great host'? Sir Ifor Williams has argued that it is.[2] He emphasises that Mynyddog's army seems to have consisted of a troop of picked and disciplined cavalry,[3] well armoured in mail coats, doubtless vastly superior tactically to what was probably an ill-armed and ill-disciplined rabble of infantry who may have been unfamiliar with such tactics (and, one might add, perhaps having a divided command). He remarks further that though in the end they were wiped out it was not before they had killed two thousand of the English 'in one hour',[4] according to verse 5 of the A. version; or seven times their own number, that is 2,100, according to verse 56 of the same. That is as may be; but without wishing to depreciate in the slightest the courage and skill of the army of Gododdin, it does seem a little far-fetched. When we remember that this is a heroic poem; that in heroic literature (which is not a military gazette) the only people who are of the slightest interest are the lords, the nobles, the 'officers', and that the rest are a mob rarely if ever mentioned; that 'infantry' in the Gododdin army are in fact spoken of as such in the Gorchan of Tudfwlch,[5] and are clearly implied

[1] If the Gododdin expedition numbered 300; if 363, then 65,340.

[2] CA., pp. xlvi ff.; on p. lv, he stresses that A.10, with its hundred thousand against three hundred, proves that 300 was the number of the whole Gododdin army, not 300 chiefs and an uncounted number of followers. But this is quite likely an aspect of the way in which the ordinary common soldier is regularly ignored in heroic poetry, as noted below.

[3] On the evidence for this see § 9 below. On cavalry in Dark Age Britain see also the Appendix, no. 7.

[4] Or, 'at one time'.   [5] Line 1295 of CA.

in the descriptions of the battle;[1] that in the later Middle
Ages at any rate (since we have no information on the Dark
Ages) the mounted knight was invariably accompanied
to war by a band of his retainers most of whom were footsoldiers; when we consider all this, it does seem probable
that we must reckon that 'three hundred' means three
hundred picked chiefs, 'knights', each of whom would
have with him a sufficient complement of supporting footsoldiers. In fact A.41 does speak precisely of three hundred
chiefs (unbenn), and A.24 mentions the hero Buddfan's 'chief
warriors', as if he brought a number of his retainers with
him. Moreover, there are several passages, such as A.25,
which show that the men in question were lords of some
importance, with 'courts' of their own, and it is most unlikely that such people would join an army like Mynyddog's without each bringing with him a contingent of his
own men. There are various other phrases, too, suggesting
that the heroes mentioned by name had their followers
with them, e.g. in A.84, 'Geraint, his battle-cry was raised
in front of the men of the South.'

How large an army all this would make one can only
guess, but anything up to three thousand or more would
perhaps be reasonable – as it would also be a great deal
more reasonable in another sense. Of course, Mynyddog
would not have feasted all these in his hall, but only the
'officers'. If so, an attempt on his part to do what the king
of Dál Riada tried unsuccessfully to do soon afterwards
with, in Bede's words, 'an immense and mighty army', even
if that had not included skilled and well-armed cavalry,
would probably not be wholly absurd. A planned force of
three thousand might have been felt to stand some chance,
granting their tactical and other superiority, against the
probable size of the hosts of Bernicia and Deira. It is unlikely in any case that these could really have numbered
the fifty-four thousand of the B. text, and still less likely a

[1] See below, § 9.

hundred thousand, an obvious poetic exaggeration.[1]

In *Canu Aneirin*, p. lvii, Williams would support the figure of three hundred by referring to a passage in an early Welsh text which says, of three royal dynasties of southern Scotland, 'The three hundred swords of the offspring of Cynfarch and the three hundred shields of the offspring of Cynwyd and the three hundred spears of the offspring of Coel, whatever expedition they undertook with one accord, that did not disappoint them.' He adds that three hundred was the standard number of a *teulu*, the picked bodyguard of a Dark Age chief, in early texts of this sort. But the numbers constituting a *teulu* do not really seem to have been fixed, still less fixed at three hundred; compare the discussion of the subject by Sir J. E. Lloyd,[2] in whose opinion 'it might number as many as one hundred and twenty'. Even if the three hundred who went to Catraeth were simply Mynyddog's regular standing *teulu* – and this is hardly consistent with the view that they were recruited for the expedition from many regions – it is still no argument for believing that the army was no larger; quite the contrary, for a *teulu* was not at all the same thing as the whole royal army, it was merely a relatively small troop who formed the hard core of such an army and acted as 'life guards' to the king – as Lloyd says, 'a body of horsemen, fed, clothed, and mounted by the king and in constant attendance on him'.

There is, however, a popular idea that cavalry were able to work wonders against infantry, and if so, that a force of

---

[1] It is worth noting as a parallel that the battles of the Civil War were mostly small affairs. According to A. Burne and P. Young (*The Great Civil War*; London, 1959, p. 14) 'a strength of 5,000 constituted a respectable army'. But if anyone is tempted to quote the charge of the six hundred of the Light Brigade they should remember that this was not a planned strategic attack on an army but a tactical move with a limited objective, the spiking of some Russian guns, and moreover was regarded as suicidal even at the time.

[2] HW., I, 316.

three hundred horsemen could well defeat a huge army of footsoldiers. A good deal of this is perhaps due to R. G. Collingwood, who, in the course of a rather highly-coloured passage about the effectiveness of cavalry under the late Roman Empire,[1] asserts that 'in 378 the battle of Adrianople had proved that a charge of heavy cavalry could roll up and destroy a vastly superior force of the best Roman infantry'; and he appears to think that the Romans thereafter laid much greater weight themselves on cavalry as a main arm. The fact is, however, that Ammianus,[2] the chief source for Adrianople, gives no real warrant for this view of the battle, but makes it clear that though during its course a portion of the Roman army was routed by a charge of Gothic cavalry *and footsoldiers*, the rest fought stubbornly until night, when at last they broke. As to the Romans being now converted to the merits of cavalry, they had in fact made considerable use of mailed cavalry ever since the time of Hadrian, with very varying success. On this, an article in *The Journal of Roman Studies*, LVII (1967), pp. 161 ff., by J. W. Eadie, should be consulted; he shows that the record of Roman cavalry in the fourth century was not impressive, and notes (p. 173) that 'the Roman experiments with mailed cavalry . . . ended in failure'. Compare also E. A. Thompson, *The Early Germans* (Oxford, 1965), p. 118, 'Although Ostrogothic cavalry took a decisive part in the struggle, Adrianople in fact was a victory of Visigothic infantrymen over Roman infantrymen.' His chapter IV should be read in connection with the questions of tactics and armament at Catraeth, and see p. 129, 'The decisive battle of Vouillé in 507 . . . represented . . . a victory of infantry over cavalry.'[3]

[1] RBES., p. 322.
[2] XXXI, 7, 10 ff.; see particularly 13. The classic study on Adrianople is that by W. Judeich in the *Deutsche Zeitschrift für Geschichtswissenschaft* VI (1891), 1 ff.; see pp. 17 f.
[3] I should like to thank Professor Charles Thomas for drawing my attention to Eadie and Thompson.

The truth seems to be that a relatively small, well-disciplined troop of heavy cavalry, without supporting infantry, might defeat a much larger body of infantry granted suitable conditions, such as that the enemy were taken by surprise, were ill-disciplined, ill-led by incompetent commanders, caught on level ground, lacking archers, and liable to make tactical blunders exposing them to devastating charges. But cavalry cannot do miracles – cannot, for instance, attack up a slope too steep for horses – and particularly, heavy cavalry cannot easily cope with infantry once they are unhorsed. With luck, a body of three hundred horsemen might win a snap victory over far greater forces. But we must remember that Mynyddog's men were apparently not a scouting troop which thought they had caught the English at a disadvantage; they seem to have been a planned expedition which had been carefully prepared for a year, and a commander who in such circumstances relied on luck, and on the utter incompetence of his future enemy, would have been quite unfit for his post, and the whole expedition would have been patently suicidal. After all, the English must have had ample warning, and could gather the men of two kingdoms; and even if the Britons were expert horsemen, their tactics cannot have been unexpected. All this is in the air, of course, because the true facts are not known; but if one believes that Mynyddog really had only three hundred horsemen, and no infantry, one cannot but feel that the whole idea was madness.

§ 5
The Men of Mynyddog's Retinue

Turning now to the poem itself, we learn very little from the people and places named in it. Scarcely any of these are known from other sources, and it will be suggested below that this is an argument for authenticity. The difficulty is, however, that owing to the obscurities of the language it is not always easy to tell what is and what is not a name. Mostly each verse not commemorating the army as a whole praises some one particular warrior, whom it names, generally at the end; but in some verses no name at all appears now to be preserved, and we are in a quandary in a case like verse 12 of the A. text, where the MS. reading *neirthiad*, meaning on the face of it 'the strengthener' (in which case no hero's name is given), is nevertheless quite probably an unrecorded personal name. Analogous difficulties apply to place-names. In addition to the eleven identifiable places already mentioned (including Gododdin, Bernicia, and Deira), plus the river Aled in Rhufoniog, there are at least seventeen others, certainly or possibly place-names but unidentified, of which one or two appear to be in the Catterick region itself. Setting aside names like Aneirin the author; Arthur the famous king of long before; Cyny, Dinogad, Dyfnwal Frych, Godebog, Myrddin, Nwython, and Senyllt, which belong to other periods or other cycles of story; and three or four (including 'Neirthiad') which may or may not be names; we have some eighty names of members of the Gododdin army (not all men of Gododdin, as we have seen), plus those of twenty-four of their fathers, one grandfather, one probable ancestor, and one contemporary (and his father's name) who was associated with Aneirin but apparently not at the battle. Out of all these, two are mentioned in early Welsh sources quite outside the *Gododdin*, and four others may be. The best identified is Cynon son of Clydno of Eidyn who is mentioned with his father's name in A.57; A.34 and 36, which give simply 'Cynon', belong to the same series as 57, so that he is likely to be the same person. In B.39 and its variant A.65 he is called 'of Aeron',[1] which would

---

[1] Cynon 'avenger of *Arfon*' in B.23 is very likely the same, with *Aeron* replaced by a Welsh scribe by the similar and more familiar *Arfon* (opposite Anglesey); easily misreading *airon* as *aruon*. But a

make his immediate origin Ayrshire if he is the same; and
the Cynon given along with 'Cynri and Cynrain of Aeron'
in A.18, and as one of the three who escaped from Catraeth
together with 'the two battle hounds of Aeron' in A.21,
appears to be the same person (on Cynon in the Gorchan
of Cynfelyn see below). In the early Welsh 'Triads' 'Cynon
son of Clydno' is one of the 'Three Lovers of the Island of
Britain', his sweetheart being a daughter of Urien (of
Rheged); and the genealogies of the Welsh saints make him
a brother-in-law of a grandson of Urien, so that for what
they are worth these items of evidence would put his floruit about 600.[1] Later he found his way anachronistically
into Arthurian romance. His father Clydno of Eidyn belonged to the latter part of the sixth century according
to a rather doubtful tradition in the Black Book of Chirk;[2]
like his son, he too appears sporadically in later Welsh
story. The other person certainly, or virtually certainly,
spoken of independently in Welsh legend is the Gwlyged
of Gododdin who is said in A.32 to have provided the
feast of Mynyddog and was therefore perhaps his steward;
his name is mentioned again in A.81. He appears in the
Mabinogion story of *Culhwch and Olwen* as Gwlgawt of
Gododdin, the owner of a marvellous drinking-horn; but
this is a 'fairy tale', and the passage preserves nothing of
him apart from his name and possibly a faint memory of
his function. In any case it throws no light on his date.
The same is true of one of the much more doubtful four,
the Bradwen of verses B.5 (= A.40) and A.41, which are
in praise of one Morien, and B.7 (= A.51) on one Addonwy (A.51 also speaks of Morien); Bradwen is mentioned in passing in all of these. A Bradwen son of Moren

---

Cynon is mentioned together with Teithfyw of Anglesey in Gorchan
Tudfwlch, though such juxtapositions prove little.

[1] Cf. TYP., p. 323 f.
[2] See ibid., p. 309 f.

Mynog is given in the list of King Arthur's wonderful men
in *Culhwch and Olwen*, and further on in the list a Bradwen
appears as brother of a Moren; but these and the scores of
other names in that list are a rag-bag of persons traditional
and imaginary, native and foreign, drawn from every con-
ceivable source known to the teller, and even if this is the
same person (in which case the Arthurian connection is
an anachronism) it tells us nothing. In the *Gododdin* there
is nothing to show the relation between Bradwen and
Morien. The doubts about the remaining three are somewhat different. In A.80 an anonymous 'son of Ceidio'
appears. Now, for what it is worth, this is not a common
name; but a famous son of a Ceidio was Gwenddolau,
a prince of south-western Scotland who was killed at
the battle of Arfderydd in Liddisdale in 574. The early
genealogies give him two brothers, Nudd and Cof, and it
would of course be chronologically possible that one of
these was the 'son of Ceidio' of A.80. Then again, A.74
speaks of 'the land of Pobddelw', which is an exceedingly
rare name – again for what this is worth; and the Old
Welsh genealogy of the kings of the country of Dunoding
in Gwynedd does give a Pobddelw, who would probably
have been very young about 600 if it is reliable.[1] It is
possible, then, that the anonymous hero of this verse might
have been one of the Gwynedd men on the expedition.
Lastly, a Cenau son of Llywarch appears in A.46, but not
as having taken part in the expedition; instead, the poet
represents him as having rescued him from captivity (a
question discussed in § 6). Now Urien of Rheged had a
first cousin Llywarch, who became very famous in later
Welsh saga tradition, which represents him, among other
things, as being present at the fight where Urien was killed

---

[1] But the date of the coming of his ancestor Cunedda to North
Wales is very uncertain; compare H. M. Chadwick, ES. p. 4, n. 1,
and p. 148; and Ifor Williams, *Transactions of the Cumberland and
Westmorland Antiquarian and Archaeological Society*, n.s. LI (1950), 77.

and as having twenty-four sons, one of whom was named precisely Cenau. The reliability of these names is questionable,[1] but certainly a nephew of Urien would belong to exactly the right generation. It is clear, then, that out of the very many names of warriors and others given in the *Gododdin* only one can be identified and dated from independent sources with any high probability, but that this, and also those of the less certain characters to whom a date can be given, is consistent – or not inconsistent – with the period about 600.

§6
Aneirin and his Date

Here we must consider the author of the poem and his date. The manuscript begins 'This is the *Gododdin*; Aneirin sang it.' The poet speaks of himself, though not by name, two or three times. In A.21 it says 'None escaped but three, through feats of combat; the two battle-hounds of Aeron, and Cynon the stubborn (?) – and I, with my blood streaming down, for the sake of my brilliant poetry' (that is, his escape is attributed to a sort of divine intervention because he was a poet). But the version that three men got away, not one, is probably not original, as we shall see (§ 7). In B.20 he says, speaking of the retinue of Mynyddog killed at Catraeth, 'I have lost too many of my true kinsmen', which implies that he himself was a Gododdin man. In A.45 and 46 there is an obscure and rather suspect episode which appears to tell that 'I, Aneirin' was captured and imprisoned (at Catraeth? which is hardly consistent with A.21) but was rescued by force by Cenau son of Llywarch.[2] The Gorchan of Cynfelyn gives a version of the tale of the three survivors – 'None came back but three,

---

[1] They include also Pyll, another rare name, and A.31 does in fact mention a Pyll, but not the name of his father.
[2] See § 14.

Cynon and Cadraith and Cadlew of Cadnant, and I after my bloody fall, the true son of prophecy; they ransomed me with pure gold and steel[1] and silver.' Here Aneirin seems to have been bought out rather than rescued. Apart from these references in the first person, there is a verse, B.2=A.52, in which some later reciter of the *Gododdin*, beginning his performance,[2] refers to its author. The archaic B. text *starts* with this,[3] as is perfectly natural in a reciter's preface, but it has got badly misplaced in the later A. text. He speaks of the poem as 'the song of the son of Dwywai', and adds 'Since the courteous one, the rampart of battle, was slain, since the earth covered Aneirin, poetry and the men of Gododdin are now parted' (the variant in A.52 is 'The slaying of the gentle one, the killing of the courteous one, the rampart of battle – Aneirin and his poetry were not to be parted'). Thus Aneirin, called the son of Dwywai, remembered for his courtesy and courage, has been killed, and all poetry in Gododdin has come to an end – or in the A. version, his poetry lives on, and his own fame with it. In the early Welsh narrative tradition represented by the Triads we are told, in fact, that one Heidyn son of Enygan killed 'Aneirin of the flowing verse, prince of poets'; a variant says he struck him on the head with a chopper.[4]

Aneirin is well known in later Welsh tradition, both as the author of the *Gododdin* and otherwise.[5] As to 'the son of Dwywai', Sir Ifor Williams was inclined to think this was a different person, but this seems to be because he took *a guarchan* in B.2 as 'and the lay', not 'with the lay'; but

[1] That is, presumably, valuable weapons or armour.

[2] See below, § 14.

[3] Apart from the verse on Dyfnwal Frych which it is agreed is an interpolation.

[4] See TYP., p. 70 f. For Heidyn see op. cit., p. 405; if a Heidyn *is* mentioned in A.75, which is doubtful, he could hardly be the same person, since the story of the *Gododdin* would demand that he must have fallen at Catraeth.

[5] References, see TYP., p. 272 f.

it can equally well bear this second meaning, and the context surely shows it must do so.[1] Nothing is known otherwise of Aneirin's parentage,[2] but Dwywai is known elsewhere both as a man's name and as a woman's, though the best evidence is for the second. The mother of St Deinioel, who is said to have founded the church of Bangor on the Menai Strait, and died according to the *Annales Cambriae* in 584, is reported by the Welsh genealogies to have been 'Dwywai daughter of Lleennog'. This would make her sister of Gwallog, one of the heroes of the North who was present, according to Nennius, at the seige of Lindisfarne and is known elsewhere in early Welsh story.[3] If so, and if this Dwywai *was* also mother of Aneirin (and of course there is nothing to show this), this would put him in exactly the right generation for the battle of Catraeth. But the oldest reference to him outside the poems in our manuscript, and the best known, is of course the passage in Nennius' *Historia Brittonum* chapter 62, where Nennius makes him a contemporary of Taliesin, and apparently of Ida, whose reign in Bernicia was probably 558–70.[4] This would put him a little earlier than one would expect, though he could well have been quite old at the time of Catraeth, say in his fifties, and could therefore already have been known as a young poet in Ida's time. But in any case the passage may well refer, not so much simply to Ida but to the whole period of the very early kings of Bernicia in the sixth century which Nennius is here discussing. This testimony to the real existence and date of Aneirin, in an

---

[1] This was also Mrs Bromwich's view, TYP., p. 272.

[2] In CA., p. 373, Williams suggests very tentatively that *mab coel* or *mab coelcerth* in the Gorchan of Cynfelyn (CA. l. 1408) means that Aneirin's father was called Coel, but other interpretations are possible and it is very doubtful.

[3] See TYP., p. 375 ff. The theory that he belonged to Elfed (see CT., p. xxxvii) is highly doubtful, since the interpretation of the line of verse on which it depends is uncertain.

[4] See Kirby, op. cit., p. 526.

author writing early in the ninth century, is of the first importance.

§ 7

How Many Came Back from Catraeth?

Before leaving the subject of the Britons present at the battle of Catraeth two further details must be treated. First, who did escape? The version which makes the army three hundred is much the better supported, being found in B.8, 9, 20=A.60, and A.8, 10, 41, and 59. There is a variant in B.9 and A.18 that it was three hundred and three ('three hounds[1] and three hundred'), though B.9 had already said three times that it was simply three hundred; and A.18 names the three as 'Cynri and Cynon and Cynrain of Aeron'. But as Williams notes,[2] this must mean that here the poet is thinking of the leaders of three divisions of a hundred each, and speaks of them separately from their followers instead of as part of them, meaning, as it were, $(99 + 1) \times 3$, not really $(100 + 1) \times 3$. According to B.8 and B.20=A.60, and A.59 and 76, only one man escaped.[3] It is nowhere stated who the one survivor was. In A.65 it says 'Of all who went to Catraeth, there came from among the Britons no man better than Cynon,' and Sir Ifor takes this to mean that Cynon was the one.[4] The version of 303 above, and also the three survivors discussed below, would certainly support this, but the fact is that the text says 'came', not 'escaped'; that is, 'sprang from', or perhaps 'came with the rest of us to Catraeth', not 'came back from'. Moreover, the B.39 version of this verse, superior in principle, has 'rare in battle was a man from among the Britons'

[1] That is, heroes.
[2] CA., p. liv.
[3] On the passage at the ends of A.2 and A.68 see the note on A.2.
[4] CA., p. liv; on p. lviii he only says he *thinks* it was Cynon.

for the 'there came from the Britons no man', and Williams himself admits that this last may be a later variant of b.39. However, the tradition of the later Welsh entertainers seems to have been that Cynon was buried at 'Rheon Rhyd',[1] which may (or may not) be near Loch *Ryan* in Wigtownshire,[2] and in any case is hardly likely to be at Catraeth, so that this suggests he did get away.[3] The other account, that 'three men and three score and three hundred' was the number of the host, is not found in the archaic b text at all, but only in a.21 and the Gorchan of Cynfelyn (plus its obviously late rubric), once each; the passage in the Gorchan is clearly a verbal echo of the one in a.21. This has every appearance of being a late and secondary elaboration of the kind beloved of antiquarians – 'three *ones*, and three *score*, and three *hundred*' – and therefore an interpolation at some later date.[4] It is notable that the authority is poor compared with that for 'three hundred'. In this version, three men came back, plus the poet, as we have seen; the idea that there were three in addition to the three hundred is already visible in b.9 and a.18 as described above, but the elaboration of the number of the army by threes seen here could well have led to multiplying the survivors without that. a.21 gives them as 'the two battle-hounds of Aeron and Cynon the stubborn', and the Gorchan of Cynfelyn as 'Cynon and Cadraith and Cadlew of Cadnant' (place unknown). It is notable that Cynon, doubtless the son of Clydno of Eidyn, is common not only

---

[1] See TYP., p. 324.   [2] See CA., p. lviii.

[3] In my article on St Kentigern in SEBC., p. 283, I have said, by one of those astonishing inadvertencies into which everyone is sometimes liable to fall, that Ywain son of Urien was one of those who escaped at Catraeth. I meant Cynon son of Clydno, of course, and cannot account for this peculiar lapse, which I take this opportunity of correcting.

[4] If there was any evidence for the 'long hundred' of 120 in Welsh this would be three 'hundreds' plus three leaders; but so far as I know there is not. There is a homonymous *cant* 'troop', but it is obvious that this would be out of place here among these figures.

to these two passages but also to A.18, and that Aeron is specifically mentioned in two of the three; but whether the 'two battle-hounds of Aeron' are 'Cynri and Cynrain of Aeron' or 'Cadraith and Cadlew of Cadnant' cannot be known, and evidently a discrepancy has arisen even within the later, secondarily elaborated account, perhaps due to a lapse of memory on the part of a reciter.

§ 8
The Party from North Wales

The other remaining problem about Mynyddog's men is the presence of a contingent from North Wales. That Mynyddog's crusade should have attracted people from parts of southern Scotland outside his domains, like Aeron, or from Pictland, or even one from Elfed in the Pennines, is not at all surprising, but one hardly expects the compact and clearly sketched little party from Gwynedd. At first sight one is tempted to conclude that the passages in which these people occur are interpolations added after the poem had come south from Scotland to Wales; but a different explanation is more probable. In A.19 it is said of Cydywal son of Sywno that he led the men of Gwynedd; of Cynfelyn in his Gorchan, that Gwynedd was his land; and of an unnamed warrior in A.73 that he was the 'liegeman' and 'steadfast one' of Gwynedd. More particularly, we have Teithfyw of Anglesey in the Gorchan of Tudfwlch, and if the Pobddelw of A.74 is really the one proposed above, an unidentified warrior from his land, Dunoding. Even better, two men in particular are well located; Gorthyn son of Urfai 'of the blood of Cilydd',[1] 'lord of the men of Gwynedd', who is twice said to belong to Rhufoniog, and to be 'seen around the Aled'; and Tudfwlch son of Cilydd (and therefore probably a close relative of Gorthyn), mentioned

---

[1] B.4; the variant A.86 makes him 'Garthwys son of Erfai of the blood of Clyd', but A.13 supports Cilydd, and N.B., in the A. version.

several times in the *Gododdin*[1] and praised in a whole
gorchan, in which last his death is said to be lamented by
'[the men of] Eifionydd', which was part of Dunoding,
and associated there also with a place Tal Hen Ban which
is evidently in Eifionydd.[2] Now, in his chapter 62 Nennius
tells us how a certain Cunedda came to Gwynedd from
the western province of Gododdin called Manaw, and expelled the Irish interlopers who had been settled there;
and early Welsh historical tradition traces back the royal
lines of several of the northern and central Welsh kingdoms
to him via his sons, including Dunoding named from his
son Dunod and Rhufoniog named from his son Rhufon.
There are various obscurities about the story, including the
date of this event,[3] and the sons and grandson given in the
Old Welsh genealogies as founding kingdoms may well be
eponymous inventions. Nevertheless the story is generally
regarded as authentic, broadly speaking; and it would be
by no means unnatural that when the king of Gododdin
was appealing widely for recruits against the English, perhaps a century and a half later, some footloose warriors
who traced their descent, or that of their king, from an
earlier lord himself hailing from Gododdin should answer
the call. This is quite compatible with believing that in
later times the tradition of the poem in Wales gave special
prominence to the Gwynedd men.

§9
Military Tactics and Equipment

Although the poems are elegies and not narrative, they do
tell us, incidentally, something about various aspects of the
life and 'material culture' of the men of Gododdin, or at
least as these were seen through the eyes of the author. To
take first the question of tactics and equipment, we have
already seen that the entire force has been thought to have

[1] B.14, 36; A.13, 15.   [2] See CA., p. 354.   [3] See p. 21, n. 1.

been a disciplined troop of cavalry.[1] There are many references to riding horses, but some of these must be set aside because it is not clear that they imply fighting on horseback. The men had a long way to go from Edinburgh to Catterick, and there would be nothing in the least anachronistic about their riding to the battle and then dismounting and fighting on foot; this would be common practice. But there remains a nucleus of passages which can only be explained by supposing that some, if not all, of the army were mounted fighters. Of these, some could be taken to refer to scattered individual horsemen in an army of infantry. Thus in B.10 it is said of the hero that 'on the day of combat he would do feats of arms, riding his white steed'; in B.18 = A.26, he hurls many spears from horseback; in B.28, he defends Gododdin on his horse 'in the forefront of battle'; in A.38 and 53 'he showered his blades between the two armies, the distinguished horseman, in front of the men of Gododdin'. But allowing for these, there are still other expressions which can only apply to a group of cavalry. So in B.16, 'there were bloodstained troops of horses and men before the men of Gododdin'; B.17, there were 'horses in the van of battle'; in B.21 we have 'the retinue of Gododdin on rough-maned horses . . . attacking the troop in the van of the host'; A.36, 'very swift were his horses, he charged before all'; A.75, 'battle horses bore bloodstained battle-harness, a red herd at Catraeth'; A.83, 'an assault of men and horses'; A.85, 'he led the horses, very swift in fight'. It will be noticed that none of these are inconsistent with there having been Gododdin infantry present also, and that B.16 and particularly B.21 can well be taken to imply it. In A.35 it is said of Morien that he 'set fire under the fleeing horseman', meant either figuratively, or perhaps more literally that he caused their horses to strike sparks from their shoes in flight; but in either case this might seem to mean that the

[1] See the Appendix, no. 7.

English had cavalry too. This however is very unlikely, and one should probably envisage, rather, that having ridden to battle and dismounted to fight, as already described, the English soldiers retreated to their horses and fled in panic on horseback.

On the other hand there does seem to be positive evidence that the army of Gododdin included infantry. In the Gorchan of Tudfwlch[1] the word is actually used, *pedyt*. Besides this, several passages distinctly suggest ranks of infantry drawn up in clusters or 'squares', making a protective rampart with their shields and a bristling hedge with their spears – like the famous 'schiltrons' at Bannockburn, a typical tactic for a weaker infantry force which is attacked by a stronger one either of infantry or cavalry. The wall of shields is familiar in Anglo-Saxon heroic poetry, the *bord-weal* or *scyld-burh* as it was called. So B.11 = A.23 tells us the hero used 'to form the [battle]-pen in the presence of the spears'; B.16 refers to defence 'in front of the battle-square (lit. 'the enclosure') of Merin'; A.14, 'in his battle-square (? lit. perhaps 'cattle-pen') he was a fence of shields,' i.e. when his men drew themselves up in a square he alone was as good as a whole rank forming a shield-wall; A.76, 'he set up a stronghold in the face of battle', i.e. drew up a 'square'; A.86, 'the gravel of the enclosure (i.e. 'square') is red.' In A.84 it is said of Geraint 'well did he attack . . . the bristling wood [of spears]',[2] which suggests the same tactic on the part of the enemy.

Whether cavalry or infantry, the army of Gododdin was a disciplined force, not a mob, as we can see from several instances of the word *dull* 'rank, array' and derivatives of it, as well as numerous references to the van, the wings, and to a warrior's 'post' in battle. B.13, 'he marshalled a

---

[1] CA. l. 1295.
[2] Cf. in *Marmion*, Canto 34, 'The stubborn spear-men still made good Their dark impenetrable wood, Each stepping where his comrade stood The instant that he fell.'

bright shining array, . . . he was in charge of a hundred
men'; A.6, 'drawing themselves up in ranks'; A.82, '[his]
rank did not flee'; A.84, 'who was wont to draw himself
up with the men of Argoed'. A passage in A.9, *dwys dengyn
yd emledyn,* literally 'compactly and stubbornly they fought',
seems a good description of infantry drawn up in massed
ranks, grimly defending their position. Instances of 'the
van, the front rank, the forefront', always a position of
honour, are many and tell us nothing (it is interesting to
note the total silence about the 'rear', or about reserves).
For the individual's special station, A.10 says 'his was the
bravest station in combat, in front of the retinue of Mynyddog'; A.29, he used to defend his post'; A.83, 'in a privileged position in conflict on the day of battle'. Early
Welsh poetry often calls a hero a 'pillar' or 'column',
meaning he upheld and supported his men by his presence
and resoluteness; so in A.7, 'the pillar of battle', and in the
Gorchan of Cynfelyn[1] 'the pillar of [battle]-fury'. A pre-
arranged tactical manoeuvre seems indicated by A.8, 'three
hundred fighting according to plan'. The *charge* is spoken
of several times; both that of a body of men and that of
the individual hero, who may or may not be leading such
a body. So B.32, 'when warriors rush forwards in the army';
A.5, 'a leader charging forwards before armies'; A.70, 'he
charged foremost before a hundred men'; A.31 gives a list
of eleven men 'who rushed forwards in battle among
broken shields'. In Celtic warfare a traditional position for
combat, particularly the typical preliminary of single combat between opposing champions, was at a ford (cf. B.17),
and there is an obscure passage in A.17 which may refer to
this. When the army bivouacked, tents were used, probably
by the chiefs alone; A.2, 'when he used to come back to
Madog's tent'.

The offensive weapons of the men of Gododdin are
swords and spears, for which latter there are several

[1] CA., l. 1397.

apparently synonymous words doubtless really expressing
varieties such as javelins thrown, spears or pikes held in
the hands of the infantrymen, and cavalry lances.[1] Throw-
ing javelins are quite clearly referred to in B.18 = A.26,
A.10, 23, 38 = 53, and the Gorchan of Cynfelyn (CA., l.
1398). The shafts are twice referred to as made of ash, the
standard wood for the purpose (B.18 = A.26, and the
Gorchan of Maeldderw, CA. l. 1437), and once of holly-
wood[2] (B.17). Spear-heads with sockets are mentioned in
A.9; and spears are said to be 'broken' or 'splintered', e.g.
A.29, 'with broken spears in splinters'. 'Blades', *llain*, are
often spoken of, but it is not always clear whether swords
or spears are meant. As in early Irish heroic literature,
there is no reference to bows and arrows, which the early
Celtic warriors seem not to have used. Anything of steel
such as blades and armour is described as *glas*, 'blue, grey',
or *gwrm* 'dark-blue, dark-brown'; what is referred to is
no doubt the bluish sheen often noticed on steel, so that
'blue' and 'dark-blue' respectively are probably the right
translations. 'Armour' or 'harness', *seirch*, appears, and
also mail-coats, *lluric*, a word borrowed from Latin *lorica*.
We have 'wearer of a broad mail-coat', B.26; 'three hosts
wearing mail-coats', A.18; 'bright mail-coats', A.33; 'mail-
clad [warriors]', A.59; 'his mail-coat stripping hand', A.71.
There is no mention of helmets, which seem not to have
been worn. The armament of the ordinary common soldier
in the Dark Ages was the spear and shield, and shields
play a large part. There are several words in use, and they
are constantly spoken of as being pierced or broken or
hacked very small; a warrior who brought back from a
battle a shield which had been very much hacked away
by the enemy was obviously a brave one. So B.4 and A.2,

[1] A full investigation into words expressing the whole vocabulary
of weapons, armour, clothing, etc. in early Welsh literature is much
needed; the same is true of early Irish.

[2] Compare Nad Crantail's holly-wood javelins in the Cattle Raid
of Cooley, Strachan and O'Keeffe, l. 1253 f.

'the front of his shield was pierced'; B.34, 'there did not come back of it as much as a hand could grip'; A.17, 'his shield was not [left] broad by the spears'; A.19, 'he left shields splintered and broken'; A.31, 'who rushed forwards in battle among broken shields'. A word sometimes occurring for 'shield' is *calch*, 'lime-white', referring to the Celtic custom of whitewashing shields well-known in early Irish literature. In the Gorchan of Cynfelyn we have the hero striking a shield 'through stud, through rivet, through hide(?), through plates and gold on the surface',[1] which suggests a very rich piece of armour, with gilded metal plates riveted to the wooden base over an under-skin of the usual hide covering.

§ 10

Standard of Living; 'Earning one's Mead'

Riches in clothing and ornament are pictured clearly elsewhere too, though such pictures may no doubt be rather exaggerated. Still, in view of the wealth of the more or less contemporary Sutton Hoo treasure and other early Anglo-Saxon graves we need not be too sceptical about this. 'Silken clothing' is mentioned in B.19, and purple in A.52 and the Gorchan of Tudfwlch;[2] in A.16, 'Blaen delighted in gold and purple [robes]'. Chequered, striped, spotted, or tartan cloth occurs a number of times, e.g. B.40 = A.63 and the Gorchan of Maeldderw.[3] Amber beads are seen in A.4, and gold ornaments in e.g. B.41, 'he put on gold [ornaments]'. A string of verses, A.2–5, begins with the adjective *kaeawc*, which can mean either 'wearing a coronet (or diadem)' or 'wearing a brooch'; but since diadems or coronets appear to have been quite unknown among the Celtic peoples in the Dark Ages and the large penannular brooches with swivel pins used for fastening cloaks, and gorgeously decorated, such as the famous Irish

---

[1] CA., ll. 1357–59. [2] CA., l. 1303. [3] CA., l. 1416.

Tara Brooch or the Scottish Hunterston Brooch, are familiar at the period, it seems certain that we should render *kaeawc* here as 'wearing a brooch' rather than 'wearing a coronet', though the second is the usual translation. But the piece of jewellery most characteristic of the ancient Celtic warrior is the torque, the collar of gold, well known among the Celts in the pre-Roman Iron Age and apparently having survived on the periphery of the Empire into the Welsh heroic age; though, as no actual examples from so late a period have been found, it has been suggested that this is an empty formula of archaic origin preserved in heroic poetry.[1]

Good living in the way of feasting and drinking is constantly referred to, particularly in connection with the year-long feast of Mynyddog before Catraeth. The scene, and the centre of life in the kingly household, is the great hall. The official responsible for this was the court officer or steward, the *maer* (B.12, 29); compare the note on Gwlyged above. The place of honour here was 'at the end of the couch' (*lleithic*, from Latin *lectica*), whatever that means exactly; so 'Cynon . . . sat at the end of the couch', A.36. The scene was one of some richness; '[reclining] on his cushions, Blaen used to dispense the drinking horn in his luxurious palace', A.16; 'the well-fed fire, the pine-logs blazing from dusk to dusk, the lit-up doorway [open] for the purple-clad traveller', A.52; 'he led us up to the bright fire and to the reclining (?) [seat covered with] white fleece', A.84. The hall was lit with tapers, A.15. After the feast the men slept in the hall, in the Dark Age manner well-known from Beowulf and the story of Grendel ('bedfellow of the beer-hall', the Gorchan of Maeldderw.[2]) The banqueters drank chiefly out of horns, which are frequently mentioned, but also from glass tumblers ('he

---

[1] Foster in G. Daniel and I. Foster, *Prehistoric and Early Wales* (London, 1965), p. 234.
[2] CA., l. 1423.

drank off wine from brimming glass vessels', B.10; 'as if it were sparkling wine from glass vessels', A.64; 'Tafloew would toss off a glass of mead', A.82) or from gold and silver cups ('wine and mead from golden vessels', A.21; 'his mead was contained in silver, but he deserved gold', A.64). Glass tumblers were in use in contemporary Anglo-Saxon England, and a number still survive. In the Gorchan of Tudfwlch there seems to be a reference to an alder-wood cup holding some bitter drink.[1]

Mead and wine are the drinks spoken of much the most often, particularly mead; but there is bragget in A.16, malt in A.60, and ale in the Gorchan of Tudfwlch.[2] It should be remarked that mead[3] is a bright *yellow* liquid about the colour of a good white Burgundy, must be strained to remove traces of honeycomb, is much more intoxicating than ordinary table wine, and tastes of honey with a sweet first impression and a slight but distinct after-taste of bitterness. A few of the more interesting passages are as follows: A.8, 'the pale mead was their feast, and it was their poison' (this famous quotation does not mean that the Gododdin army was too drunk to fight properly, but that they lost their lives in 'earning their mead', as explained below); A.11, 'they drank sweet yellow ensnaring mead'; A.15, 'we drank bright mead by the light of tapers, though its taste was good its bitterness was long-lasting'; A.31, 'drunk over the clarified mead, the retinue of Mynyddog'; A.32, 'they were feasted together for a year over the mead'; A.60, 'after wine-feast and mead-feast they hastened out'; the Gorchan of Cynfelyn, 'the sparkles of fine yellow mead' (CA., l. 1364). Wine is referred to less often; note, among other instances, B.20 = A.60, 'they fed together round the wine-vessel'; B.22, 'wine-fed before Catraeth'; B.26, 'a man reared and nourished on wine'.

---

[1] CA., l. 1262.   [2] CA., l. 1306.
[3] That is, if it is made according to the traditional recipe; and not the brownish variety sometimes obtainable nowadays.

In B.12 the poet says savagely, 'If the blood of all those you killed were wine you would have (?) plenty for three years and four'.

Mead plays a special part, however, in the thought of the heroic poetry of Britain in the Dark Ages. As we have seen, a king or chief supported at his court a 'war-band' or 'retinue', a bodyguard of picked and trained professional warriors whose special task it was to defend him in battle with their lives, and whose memory would be disgraced if he were killed and they had not died fighting to save him.[1] In return for this professional military service, the lord supplied them with board and lodging, weapons, presents, and the rest; and, as feasting in the great hall was the supreme form of this, it is summed up metaphorically as their 'mead'. Hence there is frequent mention of the hero 'earning his mead, paying for his mead, deserving his mead', which means simply earning his bread, carrying out his duty loyally and well. One may compare the English 'to be worth his salt'. To quote a few examples: 'Edar deserved to drink his mead', B.34; warriors are killed 'in retribution for earning their mead', B.40 = A.63; 'he deserved his horns of mead', A.35, 88; 'deserved sweet yellow ensnaring mead', A.73. 'Mead' is the stock metaphor, but the same idea is sometimes expressed of other drinks. So A.4, 'in return for wine from the drinking-horn'; and A.38, 53, and 80, 'in return for mead in the hall and drink of wine'; the Gorchan of Tudfwlch, 'In return for mead and ale the company went across their . . . boundary.'[2] It is well known that this is remarkably paralleled in Anglo-Saxon heroic poetry. In 'The Fight at Finnsburg', ll. 41–42, the poet says, 'Nor ever did squires pay better for the sweet mead than did his liegemen repay

---

[1] Compare a passage in the Black Book of Carmarthen (p. 92, l. 14), 'My bodyguard, do not flee! After your mead do not wish for disgrace!'

[2] CA., l. 1306 f.

Hnæf'; and in Beowulf, ll. 2633 ff., a warrior declares, 'I remember the time when we used to accept mead in the banqueting-hall, when we promised our lord who gave us these arm-rings that we should repay him for our war-equipment if ever straits like these befel him'. It is evident that this idea was common to the heroic poetry of Britons and English alike in the Dark Ages, though it is much better evidenced in Welsh.

§ 11
Christianity

It is noted above that the English army at Catterick is contemptuously spoken of as 'heathen'. Whether simply as an aspect of the general Romanisation which affected them in their situation on the very borders of the Empire, or whether more specifically as the result of the activities of St Ninian of Whithorn in the early part of the fifth century, there is good evidence that the Britons of southern Scotland were Christians by the sixth century. The poet prays that various warriors may go to Heaven, in B.12, 19, A.28, 29 ('may he have a welcome among the host [of Heaven] in perfect union with the Trinity'; therefore not Arians), and 81. A hero lays gold on the altar in A.33; another takes communion in B.40 = A.63; another would go more gladly to battle and be killed than to a wedding-feast or the altar, A.5; and the army is said to have gone to churches to do penance, A.6. However, apart from a couple of Biblical names among the warriors, that is about all, and it is remarkable that God himself is nowhere mentioned.

§ 12
The Northern Heroic Age

The *Gododdin* is a heroic poem, and its *gorchanau* are subsidiary heroic lays. The term is familiar to students of

comparative literature. It carries with it an implication of
a social setting; a military aristocratic society, whether of
a primitive or a more highly developed kind, in which the
real *raison d'être*, and the chief interest, of the nobility is
warfare, and for which the accepted morality is courage
and fierceness in war, generosity and liberality in peace, a
longing for fame, a horror of disgrace, and a welcome for
death in fight provided it leads to an immortal glory.
Heroic narrative is generally in verse, in which case it is
called epic, but may be in prose, as with the early Irish
hero tales.[1] The subject has been intensively studied by a
couple of generations of scholars, notably W. P. Ker,
H. M. and N. K. Chadwick, and Sir Maurice Bowra.
Some limit the term 'heroic' to epic narrative verse, but
others, more reasonably, extend it to all literature produced by and for a 'heroic' society if it illustrates these
characteristics. On this, one should consult in particular
the Chadwicks' *The Growth of Literature*, I,[2] chapters
II–VIII, and particularly pp. 37 ff. The heroic poems in
the Book of Aneirin are not narrative, as already noticed,
but are a mixture of elegy and panegyric, a type called by
the Chadwicks 'celebration poetry'.[3] Each verse of the
Gododdin either celebrates the deeds and laments the death
of some one hero (sometimes more than one; occasionally
he is anonymous), or those of the army of Gododdin as a
whole; and each of the longer *gorchanau*[4] does the same
with one single hero. The reason why Celtic literature has
produced no true verse epic is quite simple; in early times
the business of the professional poet, the 'bard', was not
entertainment by means of narrative, but precisely to
celebrate the praises of the aristocratic class in general and
of his own patron in particular. The bard was the pro-

[1] See OIT., passim.
[2] See GL. in the Abbreviations.
[3] Op. cit., p. 42.
[4] Apart from the anomalous Gorchan of Adebon.

pagandist and upholder of the whole structure of the aristocratic social order to an extent quite unknown in any other European literature.

The 'heroic' characteristics are well evidenced in the poetry here discussed, though much more incidentally than would have been the case if they had told a straight epic narrative. To illustrate the points of heroic conduct mentioned above the following examples may be quoted.[1] Courage and fierceness are praised everywhere, too often to need quotation, though one may mention B.12, 'when everyone else fled you attacked', and 'may you attain the land of Heaven because you did not flee'; A.2, 'he gave no quarter where he pursued, he would not come back from fight till the blood had flowed, like rushes he cut down the men who did not flee'; A.57, 'he slew the enemy with the sharpest blade, like rushes they fell before his hand'. It is notable that the hero gives no quarter and makes no truce or talk of truce; B.10, 'in conflict there was no truce that he would make, in the day of wrath he would not shirk the fight, Bleiddig son of Eli was a wild boar for fierceness'; A.12, 'he made a bath of blood and the death of his opponent sooner than speak of truce'; A.51, 'they slew, they gave no quarter to the Saxons'. As we have seen above, the charge, the attack, is of course praised, but it is interesting to see that stubbornness and steadfastness in battle, the virtues of the warrior on the defensive, are also sung of, as is very natural in the circumstances of Catraeth. So B.34, 'he was stubborn, with his shield hacked small, when he was thrust at he thrust'; A.43, 'he was an unyielding gate, an unyielding fortress of refuge'; A.73, 'the steadfast man of Gwynedd'. It is a 'heroic' characteristic that before battle, and particularly at a feast before it, the warrior boasts of the feats he intends to perform (his *aruaeth*, 'plan,

---

[1] For a fuller treatment of these points, and not limited to the Book of Aneirin, see the recent article by A. O. H. Jarman in BIK., pp. 193 ff.

intention', or his *amot*, 'pledge'), and he is expected to fulfil these promises. In Anglo-Saxon heroic poetry this is called his *gilþ* or various compounds of *gilþ* (the origin of the modern 'yelp') with words meaning 'speech', like *gilþ-word*. So A.3, 'his pledge was a promise that was kept'; A.13, 'no great man whose boasts were so expansive . . . sped forth to Catraeth'; A.19, 'because of his pledge he premeditated attack'; A.32, 'they were feasted together for a year over the mead, great were their boasts'. The fame of the hero is a constant subject for the poet, and *moleit*, 'praised, glorified, renowned' is a favourite epithet. As to the thirst for fame, note B.26, 'he slew a great host to win reputation, the son of Nwython slew a hundred princes wearing gold torques so that he might be celebrated'; and A.19, 'the son of Sywno (the soothsayer foreknew it) sold his life that his glory might be told forth'. In B.4 it is said that Gorthyn's fame 'brought visiting throngs'; and the indispensability of the bard in connection with this is well shown in A.5, 'Hyfaidd the tall shall be honoured as long as there is a minstrel', and A.66, 'what he desired was the acclamation of bards all round the world for [his] gold and great horses and drunkenness on mead', that is, for the great state he kept up. In B.17, 'he was glad when he bore off the honoured portion in the palace' would seem to refer to a custom similar to that of the early Irish *curadmír* whereby the best and most famous warrior present was allotted the best portion of meat served at the feast.[1]

Though the hero is savage in fight he is gentle and courteous at home. Words expressive of gentle blood and breeding are used, and mild behaviour is praised. 'In [battle]-straits he struck with blades, steel weapons on the heads [of men, but] in the palace the slayer was mild', A.14; 'any lady or maiden or well-born man could approach the son of Urfai, could approach the proud boar', B.4; and 'he was civil to the suppliant', A.43. Above all, he

[1] Cf. OIT., p. 21.

is liberal – and liberality to bards is naturally looked on with favour. In A.25 Gwenabwy purposely stays at his court over the New Year, the time for giving presents, and makes gifts 'to the minstrels of Britain'; A.27, Isag is generous and luxurious – 'his manners were like the sea-flood for graciousness and liberality and pleasant mead-drinking'; A.33, Rhufon gave 'gifts and fine presents to the minstrel'; A.46, Cenau is called 'the lord who was bountiful by his nature'; A.71, 'the prince dispensed pay' to the poet himself; in the Gorchan of Cynfelyn the hero is 'the en-richer of his country',[1] and Aneirin says 'he gave me his fine gilded spear, may it be for the good of his soul'.[2]

Two other stock features may be mentioned. By killing the enemy, or being killed himself, the warrior provides food for carrion birds and beasts; so for ravens (B.38, A.1, 5, 24), for eagles (A.19, 65), and for wolves (A.30). In A.58 there is a vivid picture of 'ravens soaring and mounting to the clouds' above the battlefield. The other is that the hero is himself often compared to various kinds of savage or wild or stubborn creatures; to a lion (A.57), a bear (A.16, 62), a boar (B.4, A.30, 39, 69), a wolf (A.4, the Gorchan of Tudfwlch,[3] the Gorchan of Cynfelyn[4]), a stag (A.84), an ox (A.39), a bull (A.30, 37, 38, 48, 53, 73, the Gorchan of Tudfwlch[5]), a serpent (A.62), an eagle (A.40, 49, 85), a hawk (A.69), or a dragon[6] (B.3, A.22, 25).

§ 13
The Text

The manuscript called the 'Book of Aneirin' and contain-ing the *Gododdin* and the *gorchanau* is now in the Free

[1] CA., l. 1375.
[2] CA., l. 1393 f.
[3] CA., l. 1278 f.
[4] CA., l. 1399.
[5] CA., l. 1286.
[6] See the sensible remarks on this in TYP., pp. 93 ff.

Library at Cardiff, where it is numbered 'Cardiff 1'. It is a
vellum, and is written in two contemporary hands of about
the year 1250, christened by Williams 'A.' and 'B'. It has
38 pages as it now stands, but the text breaks off in the
middle of a word at the bottom of p. 38, and there were
once at least three more vellum folios, that is, six pages,
since the stumps of these remain where they have been cut
off.[1] Whether there were ever still further folios we shall
never know, or not unless a better MS. is one day dis-
covered. The history of the hands is as follows. The hand
A. wrote the first twenty-two pages and as far down p. 23 as
line 5; it left the rest of p. 23, and all p. 24, blank, but
began again at the top of p. 25 and continued as far as half
way down p. 30, where it stopped. Then B. came along,
and wrote another copy of verses, filling the gap on pp. 23
and 24 and carrying on from the second half of 30 to the
end of the MS. as we now have it, though it is clear it had
continued further on to the first lost page at least – how
much further one cannot say. What A. wrote on pp. 1–23
was eighty-eight verses of the *Gododdin*; when he started
again on p. 25 he wrote out the four *gorchanau*, which took
him as far as the top half of p. 30, after which he wrote no
more. It looks as if he knew that there was more of the
Gododdin to be had than was accessible to him up to the
present, and left a space in which he hoped to enter this
later, presumably believing it to be adequate; but never
completed the task. The hand B., however, did know more,
indeed a different text of the *Gododdin*, and what he did
was to write this into the MS. after A. had finished with it,
first filling the gap with six verses, and then picking up
again on the blank pages after the *gorchanau*.

The text which B. gives is much more archaic in its
spelling, and to some extent its language, than A.'s. As
Williams has demonstrated, the spelling of the B. text shows
quite clearly that it was copied, either directly or at one

---

[1] Cf. G. Morgan in BBCS., XX, 12 ff.

or more removes, from a lost manuscript in Old Welsh; that is to say, written at some time between the end of the eighth century and the end of the eleventh, though most probably in the ninth or tenth,[1] since features peculiar to the eighth and eleventh are missing. Hand B. does begin by modernising the spelling to some extent, in the direction of his own thirteenth-century orthography, though leaving unaltered particularly archaic words which he did not recognise; but he gets tired of this, and by about his verse 17 (and sporadically before) he is giving it up. A.'s text, however, is almost wholly in the spelling of his own day, and it is likely that he was copying a much later MS. than the one B. used, the product of further centuries of written evolution, which required much less modernisation. Nevertheless the A. text itself sometimes provides misreadings which point to the miscopying of a written source, somewhere in the line of filiation, in the 'Hiberno-Saxon' handwriting of the Old Welsh period.

Not only is most of the orthography of the B. text archaic, but there are numerous archaic features about the language of the poems, particularly the B. text. There is no need to enter into these here; they have been discussed by Ifor Williams and Henry Lewis (see p. 59 n. 2 below). On the whole the B. text is basically more original than the A. text,[2] as well as being older, but it has undergone distinctly more decay of a certain sort, nevertheless. It is obvious that behind the Old Welsh written text from which B. derives there was a longish period of oral recitation during which a very considerable degree of corruption due to faulty memory crept in, corruption of a kind far too extensive to be due to mere miscopying of written sources. The same is true of A. too, though on the whole markedly

---

[1] Williams constantly refers to this source as 'ninth century', but strictly speaking the facts are as given above (CA., p. lxvii, he admits it may be ninth, eighth, or tenth century, and that the same spelling is seen in the *Annales Cambriae* of the end of the tenth).

[2] Cf. Williams, CA., p. xiii.

less so; the trouble with A is that it is much more modernised than B. The whole problem is one of *variants*. It is not
always easy to be sure when one verse *is* a variant of
another, since it is a common device in very early Welsh
poetry to begin a stanza with the whole, or part, of the first
line of the preceding one (and sometimes more than the
first line), and so on in the following verse or verses in a
'chain', a rhetorical device to give emphasis to a basic
thought by repetition while developing it differently in the
rest of the verse.[1] If the *whole* first line is repeated the
rhyme all through the stanza will be the same, in those
metres which have only one rhyme in each. Now, in the
Gododdin the hero of each verse tends to be named in the
last line or couple of lines, and consequently in a 'chain' of
verses commemorating one single man not only the beginning but also the end of each verse may be repeated as the
same or closely similar. In such circumstances, granting
a considerable degree of oral corruption in the handing on,
it is not always easy to say whether stanza x is a variant,
a badly remembered version, of stanza y, or whether it is
simply another link in a single 'chain'.

Allowing for this, some fourteen of the forty-two verses
of the B. text fairly clearly have close variants, that is, are
repeated in a closely similar form, in the A. text, and
another five have partial variants – parts of the two verses
are essentially the same, other parts are clearly not.[2]
Further, there are two pairs of stanzas (nos. 3 and 24, and
25 and 35) which are close variants *within the B. text itself*;
and two further groups within that text, one a pair (verses
5 and 6) and one a group of four (nos. 14, 15, 16, 36) which

---

[1] This is the metrical feature called 'incremental repetition'; see
the author's study of this in early Welsh poetry in *Speculum* xvi,
304 ff.

[2] Part of a quite different verse may get inserted in or added to
another because the metre and rhyme is the same; or on the contrary,
a genuine pair of variants may be made to seem rather different by
such an addition, as in the case of B.2 and A.52.

are partial variants. There is one pair of close variant verses *within the* A. *text* (A.38 and 53), and probably one partial one (A.40 and 41), but others such as A.36 and 57 are rather members of 'chains' which have got misplaced. The fact that there are many verses in A. and B. which are clearly variants as between the one text and the other is not at all surprising, on the contrary it is exactly what would be expected with two versions of the same poem which have had a history of oral transmission; but it is highly significant that both, and particularly B., have variants within themselves, since it points clearly to a period of oral tradition behind the beginning of the written one, in each case, during which the order of the verses, and the construction of the poem, had become badly muddled. The same verses coming in a different order in the two texts mean oral displacement, but normally one cannot say in which text; thus B.1–7 are variants of A.78, 52, 48, 86, 40, 41, and 51 in that order, but it is impossible to tell which is more original – at any rate they are badly out of place in either one or the other. But when a verse clearly forms part of a chain from which, however, it is separated, it may be easier to be sure. So the chain B.39, 40, and 42 (into which 41 is wrongly inserted) appears in A. as 65, 63, and 66 respectively, these being part of a chain A.63–67; and it looks as if A. is right here. A. gives a distinctly better text than B. in all these regards, which is all the more remarkable considering it is more than twice the length of B.; but otherwise it is on the whole a much later and less original version. In the A. text with its eighty-eight verses against B.'s forty-two it is natural that a great many of them (probably sixty-four) have no variants in B.; and moreover there are several long sequences of these, the longest being A.1–19, whereas B. has very few such and the longest of them is only four verses.

All this means that while the oral version behind B. kept some parts of the original poem not known to that behind

A., the latter preserved far more of it than the former did (though a good deal of this may have been present in the lost part of B.).

§ 14
The Interpolations

An important aspect of the textual tradition of the *Gododdin* is the question of interpolations. These certainly occur, whether of whole verses or of single lines or groups of lines. Some are clearly scribal, but others have obviously taken place in the process of the oral transmission, as is only to be expected.

To take the scribal interpolations first, there are at least three cases of whole verses getting into the text in this way. The most immediately obvious is A.87, which has nothing whatsoever to do with the *Gododdin*, or even with heroic poetry either. It is a delightful cradle song to a baby called Dinogad, by its mother, who first whistles and croons to the child and summons the household slaves to do likewise, and then tells it how its father would go a-hunting with his dogs Giff and Gaff, bringing back deer or grouse or 'fish from the falls of Derwennydd'.[1] It is impossible that this should be an oral interpolation, and it must have got into the A. text owing to the scribe of some earlier MS. having jotted it down in a margin or other blank, and some later copyist having then mechanically incorporated it into the main text of the MS. he was writing, perhaps not understanding what it was about. A.87 is the last verse but one in the A. version of the *Gododdin*, and it is likely that it had been entered by the scribe of the MS. A. was copying on the

---

[1] This is identical with the modern river-names Derwent and Darwen (see LHEB., pp. 282, 353), but it is impossible to tell which of the several rivers of this name is meant, if any. There are Derwents in Co. Durham (flowing into the Tyne opposite Newcastle), the Lake Hills (with Derwent Falls), and E. Yorkshire. The first is perhaps the most likely, being within the bounds of Gododdin.

last page of *his* manuscript because there was plenty of room there. Another obvious scribal interpolation is A.44. This is an 'englyn', a three-line stanza of a metrical type of which there is only one other example in the whole poem; it is addressed to one Cyny, and belongs not to the story of Catraeth but to a quite different body of early Welsh poetry, the cycle of Llywarch Hen, whose son Cyny was. These poems are in englynion, and the present instance is not merely typical of them but is obviously an actual quotation from them, since a verse forming a close 'variant' with this one occurs in one of the poems of that cycle.[1] It is clear that this englyn likewise got into the A. text by having been entered in the margin, and that the reason why it was so entered is the fact that A.46 is addressed to Cenau son of Llywarch, another son of Llywarch Hen in his saga,[2] and this must have reminded some scribe of the verse about his other son Cyny.

Both these interpolations are found in the A. text only. A third, and an exceedingly interesting one, is seen in both. This is B.1 = A.78. It is a verse of heroic eulogy of exactly the same type as those of the *Gododdin* and in the same metre as that of the first of the two verses analysed metrically below in § 16, but it has no connection at all with Gododdin. It speaks of a battle between two forces, one apparently led by 'the grandson[3] of Nwython', and ends in ferocious glee, 'and the head of Dyfnwal Frych, ravens gnawed it'. This gives us the clue: Dyfnwal Frych, 'Freckled Donald', would be Domnall Brecc in Old Irish,[4] and in fact we know who this was – he was king of the

---

[1] See CLH., pp. 8 and 98.

[2] See CLH., p. xxx and compare p. 21 above.

[3] Ifor Williams' very plausible emendation; see *Transactions of the Cumberland and Westmorland Antiquarian and Archaeological Society*, NS. 51 (1950), pp. 80 ff. It should be noted that the identification of Dyfnwal Frych and the battle of Strathcarron does not rest on this emendation.

[4] Actually, *Domnual Brecc* in his own lifetime (the Irish *m* and the Modern Welsh *f* both mean *v*), which is still closer to the Welsh.

Scottish Gaelic kingdom of Dál Riada, and was killed by
the Britons of Strathclyde under their king Ywain at the
battle of Strathcarron near Falkirk in 642. Ywain was son
of Beli son of Neithon, and this is who is meant by 'the
grandson of Nwython'.[1] It is evident that what we have
here is a fragment of a Strathclyde bardic panegyric on
Ywain and his victory at Strathcarron, which has become
interpolated into the *Gododdin*. Part of the importance of
this lies in the fact that it confirms and proves, what one
knew *a priori* must be the case, that such poetry flourished
among the Britons of Strathclyde as among all the Celtic
peoples; and also that it shows it was essentially of exactly
the same nature as the *Gododdin*. Incidentally it is valuable
support for the view that such poems were being composed in southern Scotland in the first half of the seventh
century. The reason for thinking that this is a written
interpolation is the fact that in the B. text it is the very first
verse of all, which strongly suggests that it had been inserted in the blank at the top of the first page of an earlier
manuscript, and was incorporated as part of the *Gododdin*
by a later scribe copying this manuscript. In the A. text it
became misplaced subsequently; perhaps another scribe
copying the first manuscript realized it was a marginale,
but was sufficiently interested to insert it as such somewhere else in his copy where there was more room. The
implications of this are discussed below.

As for oral interpolations, B.2 = A.52 may well be a
case. This verse is not the work of 'Aneirin', of the original
composer, but is a prologue prefixed to the entire poem by
some subsequent reciter of it after Aneirin was dead. This
man gets up in the hall, 'in the presence of the throng in

---

[1] *Neithon* is the Brittonic form from older *Nechton*, which is also the
early Old Irish (later *Nechtan*) and Pictish (later *Neiton*); see PP.,
pp. 145, 164. *Nwython* appears to be a by-form of this which occurs
elsewhere in early Welsh tradition applied to Britons of the North,
and also in the *Gododdin* itself twice in B.26.

the court', and bases his claim to the reward for recitation on the fact that he is about to recite the *Gododdin*; Aneirin is dead, and this has been a deadly blow to poetry in Gododdin (see § 6 above). Such prologues are a well-known feature of orally recited poetry, and what has happened is that in the source of B. it was simply included in its proper place at the very beginning as part of the poem, whereas in A. it got out of place later as a result of the general tendency to re-shuffle the order through faulty memory. It is obvious that the B. text preserves better than the A. text the start of some early MS. near to the original oral poem.

Another oral interpolation of later date is very probably the version that the men who went to Catraeth numbered three hundred and sixty-three and that three escaped, instead of three hundred and one respectively, as we have already seen in § 7, arising out of a typical 'pedantic' elaboration. It is found only once in the *Gododdin*, in the A. text, once in the Gorchan of Cynfelyn, and once in the rubric which is itself an interpolation (see below). A further instance is likely to be the reference to Myrddin in A.40 – 'Morien defended the blessed inspiration of Myrddin'. A.41 is a partial variant of this verse, and B.5 and 6 are close variants of A.40 and 41 respectively, but the reference to Myrddin is in A.40 alone, and it is evident it is secondary. Myrddin is the inspired prophetic poet who found his way into the continental Arthurian romance as Merlin; as such, he belongs to a wholly different cycle of literature and to a Welsh, not a Scottish context,[1] and this has every appear-

---

[1] That is, by name. The tale of the mad prophet living in the forest and consulted by visitors about the future is a migratory legend told about various characters. It was known in Strathclyde at least as early as the twelfth century, but the hero of it here was called Lailoken. The Welsh story of Myrddin has very close connections with the Lailoken legend, which very likely came from Strathclyde to Wales, where the name of the Welsh prophet Myrddin was substituted; but there is no reason to think this happened early, and certainly not as

ance of being a later interpolation in the A. text on Welsh
soil.

Still another possible oral interpolation is the story of
Aneirin's captivity referred to briefly above in §§ 5 and 6,
and told in A.45 and 46. The speaker calls himself 'I,
Aneirin', and appears to tell a story about how he was
lying in a prison ('an underground dwelling') 'under the
feet of maggots', with a chain about his knees, and how
Cenau son of Llywarch saved him – 'by the might of his
bright sword he rescued me, from the barbarous underground prison he took me, from the place of death'. The
introduction of a personal experience of this nature seems
thoroughly out of place in this poem; besides, if it refers to
his being captured at Catraeth it is inconsistent with the
story that he escaped wounded, though more consistent
with that given in the Gorchan of Cynfelyn that he was
ransomed — this however also being a suspect passage
because it refers to the story of the *three* survivors. Moreover the cycle of Llywarch Hen has no connection with
the Gododdin tale, though certainly Llywarch's sons (if he
ever existed) would have been contemporary with Catraeth. Finally, there is an obscure reference to Taliesin in
verse 45 which again smacks of lateness; and one may also
mention that there is something to be said for the view held
by some that Aneirin is not imprisoned but dead and in
the grave, though this appears to be inconsistent with the
chain (unless this is metaphorical for a shroud) and with
his rescue; which, however, could be a later accretion
owing to a misunderstanding. The last sentence of the
verse could be a coda added by someone to claim author-
ship of the poem for Aneirin. The words 'and yet not I'
might mean 'since I am dead and do not exist' (the theme

early as the *Gododdin*. For a bibliography of Myrddin see TYP., pp.
469 ff.; and see also in particular A. O. H. Jarman, 'The Welsh
Myrddin Poems' in *Arthurian Literature in the Middle Ages* (ed. R. S.
Loomis, Oxford, 1959), pp. 20 ff.

of a poet speaking a poem after death from his grave is known elsewhere in Welsh poetry); and the author may have believed that Taliesin composed an elegy on Aneirin – may even have know such a poem. It may or may not be significant that these two verses are lacking in the B. text.

§ 15
The Gorchanau, and the Rubric

When discussing the text, a word on the *gorchanau* or 'lays' is needed. There are four; but one, fifteen lines entitled the Gorchan of Adebon, is anomalous. It appears to be a string of unconnected proverbs, and no 'Adebon' is described in it. It too is very likely an interpolation; in much later times Aneirin had the reputation of being the author of proverbial verse,[1] and if this was already the case in the thirteenth century the attribution of the poem to him would be explained.[2] The other three are heroic lays, on three of the warriors of the army of Gododdin; the lay of Tudfwlch, sixty-four lines in Williams' arrangement; the lay of Cynfelyn, seventy-five lines, and the lay of Maeldderw, sixty-nine lines. Each of these is similar in treatment to the individual verses of the *Gododdin*, and it is significant that Tudfwlch is celebrated in three verses, plus one variant, in the *Gododdin* itself.[3] These heroic lays probably represent a more original type of eulogistic poetry than the short verses of the *Gododdin*, where they had to be short or the whole would be far too long; and in this respect they are more like the very early panegyrics to Urien in the Book of Taliesin. There appears to be no special reason why these three heroes should have been chosen for this treatment. It is notable that the one on

[1] See K. Jackson, *Early Welsh Gnomic Poems* (Cardiff, second impression, 1961), pp. 12 ff.

[2] But one must reckon with the possibility that his reputation as a proverbial poet arose precisely *because* of the Gorchan of Adebon.

[3] B.14=B.36, and A.13 and 15.

Cynfelyn describes itself in ll. 1390 f. of Williams' edition as 'the Gorchan of Cynfelyn appended to the *Gododdin*', implying its secondary character, and equally striking is the fact that the long rubric appearing in the MS. between this *gorchan* and that of Maeldderw says of the latter that Taliesin composed it. If so, it has no real place in 'The Book of Aneirin'; but the authority of the rubric is very poor. In any event the *gorchanau* give the general impression of being secondary to the *Gododdin*.

What the rubric says is this: 'Every verse of the *Gododdin* is worth a whole continuous poem because of its rank in the poetic competition. Each one of the Gorchanau is worth three poems and three score and three hundred; this is the reason, because the numbers of the men who went to Catraeth are commemorated in the Gorchanau. No bard ought to go to the competition without this song any more than a man ought to go to battle without weapons. Here now begins the Gorchan of Maeldderw. Taliesin sang it, and gave to it as high a rank as to all the verses of the *Gododdin* and its three Gorchanau in the poetic competition'.

The fact that the poets of early Wales held competitions something like an eisteddfod for the recitation of poetry, apparently both new and old, in which marks were awarded according to the prestige of the poem, or its excellence, or the difficulty of its metres, and rewards were duly given, is known from other sources and confirmed by this; for instance some of the poems in the MS. of the Book of Taliesin actually have the marks noted, four with a value of '24', one of '90', and three of '300'.[1] How far these are reliable is a question, but certainly the 'marks' mentioned in the rubric are an absurdity, and the whole thing smells strongly of bogus pedantry; and the attribution of the Gorchan of Maeldderw to Taliesin is consequently suspect also.

[1] Cf. CA., p. lvii.

One thing, at any rate, which the rubric does show is that the *Gododdin* was recognized as a great bardic classic and was recited as such at competitions. It was still known by the poets of the 'period of the Princes', twelfth to fourteenth centuries. So Cynddelw composed an elegy on the household retinue of Ywain Gwynedd, king of North Wales (died 1170), with a verse or two on each of the retainers who had been killed, after a splendid feast and mead from Ywain's drinking horns – the whole obviously an echo of the *Gododdin* in general and in detail. The same applies to a celebrated eulogy of his warriors by Ywain Cyfeiliog, a Welsh prince who died in 1197; he calls on his cupbearer to pour drink from a great horn for each in turn, praising their deeds, in language again clearly reminiscent of the *Gododdin*. He actually quotes a line from it,[1] and says elsewhere, 'I have heard how the dragons[2] went to Catraeth, as payment for their mead, with their pledge faithfully kept and sharpened weapons, the retinue of Mynyddog'. So too, Dafydd Benfras, a poet of the second quarter of the thirteenth century, prays for inspiration to sing as Aneirin did when he sang the *Gododdin*. Finally one may mention the Triad of the Three Splendid Retinues,[3] in the collection of 'triads', or mnemonic references to traditional events and people of early Welsh literature conveniently grouped and codified in threes, which was probably put together more or less in the form in which we now have it in the twelfth century. The first of the three is 'The Retinue of Mynyddog of Eidyn', or in a variant version 'The Retinue of Mynyddog at Catraeth'.

§ 16
Metre

The *Gododdin* consists of a number of separate verses, of very varying length but averaging about ten lines per

[1] CA., l. 324.   [2] Lit. dragon; i.e. warrior.   [3] See TYP., p. 65.

verse. The principle of the line is not a matter of alterna-
tion of stresses, as in English poetry, but of the number of
syllables in the line; this is, or should be, fixed according to
a regular pattern, though there is some latitude which in
many cases may really be due to the imperfect preservation
of the text. Thus in some instances all the lines in the verse
have the same number of syllables, commonly ten or nine,
though there are verses with as few as four. It is usual for
verses of this type to have the same end-rhyme all through,
that is, the lines all rhyme together (this arrangement is
called *unodl* in Welsh); but less often the rhyme may
change part-way through the verse, or there may be
rhyming couplets. There may also be less regular arrange-
ments, for instance A.1, which is twenty lines of mostly five
syllables, varying with four and six; the first four rhyme in
-*as*, the next four in -*an*, the next four in -*i*, the next two in
-*awr*, the next four in -*ein*, and the last two in -*o*. There is
commonly internal rhyme (a different one) within the line,
as well as end-rhyme; if the line is at all long there is a
caesura, and the syllable in caesura will rhyme then with a
syllable either in the first half-line or in the second, or
sometimes in both. Marking the end-rhymes with capitals,
the internal rhymes with italics, and the caesura, we thus
have an example of an *unodl* verse (A.8):

> Gwyr a *aeth* Gatr*aeth*, / oed fr*aeth* eu llU,
> glasved eu hanc*wyn* / a gwen*wyn* vU;
> trych*ant* trwy beiry*ant* / en cattaU,
> a gwedy el*wch* / tawel*wch* vU; etc.

Here the lines are of nine syllables, with the caesura at the
fifth; and the end-rhyme in -*u* continues throughout the
verse.

Another common metrical arrangement, however, is a
group of three or four short lines all rhyming together by
end-rhyme (call it *a*) plus another line with a different
last syllable (call it *b*), followed by a second group of three

or four lines all rhyming *c*, plus a further line rhyming *b*; and so on without fixed limit. The line which rhymes *b* may have internal rhyme with the end-rhyme of the lines immediately preceding. So A.62, in which the lines are all of four syllables:

> Angor Dewr d*aen*,
> sarph seri r*aen*,
> sengi wr(y)mg*aen*
> e ml*aen* bedIN;
> arth arwyn*awl*,
> drussyat dreissy*awr*,
> sengi waew*awr*
> en dyd cady*awr*
> yg cl*awd* gwernIN, etc.

This could be printed in long-lines and caesuras, as follows:

Angor Dewr d*aen*,/sarph seri r*aen*,/sengi wr(y)mg*aen*/e ml*aen* bedIN, etc.

But many verses are not by any means so regular in their metrical arrangement as the above schemes would suggest, though in a good many cases this is obviously due to the imperfect preservation of the text.

In addition to rhyme there is also commonly alliteration, not as a fixed requirement as in Anglo-Saxon or Irish verse, but as a decoration which may or may not appear, according to no rule, as in English. Two alliterations to the line are common, but three or four are also found: thus, with the alliterations in capitals, CA., l. 78,

> ar deulu Brenn*eych* / B*eych* Barnasswn.

Williams has discussed very interestingly in CA. pp. lxxvii ff. the question of which consonants can alliterate with which, and the upshot of it is, in the light of more recent research on the phonology of British and early Welsh,[1] that

---

[1] See LHEB., pp. 543 ff.

some aspects of the rules on this observed in the Aneirin poems must have been quite archaic and traditional by the end of the sixth century and for over a century before that. This, however, does not mean that the date of the poems must be pushed back into the fifth century, but simply that, as in medieval Irish versification, ancient poetic rules in matters of this sort can survive, in a rigid bardic tradition of the Celtic type, long after they have ceased to have true phonetic reality. This kind of alliteration is found, as Williams shows, in other very early Welsh poems apparently belonging to the same general period, but such is the force of the bardic conservatism that traces of it are still to be seen in poetry as late as the middle of the tenth century.

§ 17

Date, Authenticity, and Transmission of the Poems

The final question is the most significant of all. What really is the date of the *Gododdin* and its additional lays? Can they be considered to belong to about the year 600, and to have been composed by 'Aneirin'? It is most striking that the events described – in so far as any can be said to be described – and all the historical background seen in the poems, suit exactly what we know about the history of the North at the very end of the sixth century, and suit no other period. Moreover, the whole tone is contemporary, not harking back to a distant past; the poet is praising and lamenting his own relatives and friends, people he knew well, whose character he describes with a personal knowledge which was no doubt shared by his listeners and was intended to appeal to them as such. Thus he tells the anecdote of Morien who tackled a wolf bare-handed (B.6 = A.41); he says it was 'usual for the son of Golistan, though his father was no great lord, that what he said was listened to' (B.28); of another hero, 'his refined manners were perfection' (A.28); of another, 'he struck with blades, steel weapons on the heads of men, but in the palace the slayer was mild' (A.14); of another, 'I know you, generous Geraint, you were noble' (A.84); and of another, 'any lady or maiden or well-born man could approach the son of Urfai' (B.4). He addresses many of them in the second person, as if they were still living (e.g. B.7, 12, 14, 15, A.20, etc). He speaks of them as friends and companions for whom he grieves personally; so, 'when my comrade was struck' (B.17); 'my heart has become full of grief for the feast of Mynyddog, I have lost too many of my true kinsmen' (B.20 = A.60); 'I have lost a friend to whom I was loyal' (A.9); 'my kinsman' (A.22); 'I know the grief for their death' (A.59); 'bereavement has come upon me unsought' (A.88); 'a year of mourning is mine for the men of Catraeth who fostered me' (Gorchan of Tudfwlch, CA. l. 1316); 'he gave me his fine gilded spear' (Gorchan of Cynfelyn, CA., l. 1393). He himself appears as having been present and a witness of it all, from the feast of Mynyddog to the disaster at Catraeth. 'Though we drank bright mead by the light of tapers' (A.15); 'I drank off mead at one draught on my journey, wine-fed before Catraeth' (B.22); 'all us kinsmen who went' (B.8); 'a second heavy grief it is to me to have seen our men falling headlong' (A.81). According to the version that three men came back from Catraeth, Aneirin himself was a fourth, who escaped wounded, but it has already been pointed out that this is probably a later accretion; anyone multiplying the original one by three might very well be moved to add the poet as well, since the poem makes it clear he too was there at Catraeth and therefore came back. This apart, the whole tone of the rest implies that the poem was in some sort the work of a contemporary.

If it was not, it is a 'forgery'; a poem in praise of people long dead, by some later poet trying to pass his own composition off as that of Aneirin, a famous bard of the old days – though one should stress that even if so, it cannot be

later than the ninth to tenth century B. text. But in the first
place it is most unlikely that anyone composing such a
poem centuries later than Catraeth could have known
enough about northern history and the men of the North
about the year 600 to have got all the historical setting
right. Again, what would have been the point of such
forgery? The purpose of bogus eulogistic bardic poems,
when they do exist, is to glorify the ancestors of the bard's
own patrons, and thus indirectly to glorify those patrons
themselves, their descendants. But in the ninth to tenth
centuries, or for that matter in the second half of the
seventh century and thereafter, there *were* no descendants
of those who were the lords and chiefs of Gododdin at the
time of Catraeth. These regions had fallen entirely into
English hands, and the princely Cumbric families of
Gododdin vanished from the scene; Mynyddog may well
have been almost its last king.[1] This is probably the reason
why virtually nothing is known of any of the heroes of
Gododdin, and why none of them (apart from a possible
case in North Wales, which is quite a different matter) left
any dynasties known and celebrated in later tradition.[2] All
this is perfectly natural if the poem is 'genuine', but it
would be nonsensical for a forger to invent such a poem.
Moreover, when bogus 'historical' poems are found in
Celtic literature praising the ancestors of chiefs whose lines
still survived, as does happen in Ireland at any rate, the
whole tone is quite different. It lacks any convincing
verisimilitude, and the falsehood is patent.

[1] Hardly its last, if he was too old to fight at Catraeth.
[2] It is highly unlikely that our hypothetical forger could have been
a bard of North Wales trying to make glorious some line of northern
Welsh kings who claimed descent from Cunedda of the Gododdin
province of Manaw, by praising the heroes of Gododdin as a whole
who lived some 150 years after his time. The Gwynedd men at
Catraeth are very few, and virtually the entire interest is concentrated
on the northerners; it is clear that the former are mentioned incidentally by a northern poet, and are not the chief centre of interest
as they would be to a southern poet.

If, then, the poems are admitted to be 'genuine', in what sense is this word used? Do we mean that every single word as we have it was composed by Aneirin? Five questions must be considered here; language, metre,[1] bardic tradition, contemporary literature of the same type, and the state of the text. Not enough is known about very early Welsh and Cumbric to be able to date the *Gododdin* and *gorchanau* with confidence on purely linguistic grounds, but the language and vocabulary are certainly very archaic, and consequently often very obscure. Sir Ifor Williams has given an analysis of some features of the language,[2] and has shown that in spite of later modernisations it is at any rate less evolved than that of the Old Welsh glosses of the ninth to tenth centuries. With regard to metrical considerations, the essential is that it is syllabic and rhyming. Celtic poetry was probably originally accentual rather than narrowly syllabic, and was heavily alliterated but without rhyme at all; specimens of this survive in Irish, though not in Welsh. The appearance of purely syllabic verse and rhyme has been believed to be of Latin origin,[3] but it is generally agreed that they had been adopted into native Celtic poetry as early as the sixth century, so that their appearance here is no bar to a date about 600. Further, Williams' discussion has shown, as we have seen, that the alliteration so common throughout presents phonological features which were already archaic by that

[1] For some criticisms of the early date in respect of these first two features see the Appendix, no. 8.

[2] CA, pp. lxiii ff. Compare also the article on the syntax by Henry Lewis in BBCS. XIII, 185 ff. There is still scope for a completely exhaustive study.

[3] But Calvert Watkins has recently made a case for the syllabic line being of Celtic origin, though admittedly influenced by Latin. The Irish eight plus seven syllable couplet in particular has close Latin parallels; but it is worth noting that the *Gododdin* has a considerable variety of syllabic metres, among which this does not figure at all. It may well be that we have here a further argument for Watkins' view that the Celtic syllabic line is essentially native.

time, and that this was purely vestigial by the tenth century.

As to the bardic tradition, we have to bear in mind that by very ancient common Celtic custom, poetry was composed in the head and without the use of writing; was recited orally to the assembled company in the chief's hall; and was handed down orally, being learned by heart by subsequent reciters and so passed on for generations; and that all this was fostered and practised by the institution of 'bardic schools' in which budding poets were given an elaborate training in their profession, in oral composition of poetry, and its recitation and transmission when learned by heart.[1] It has already been mentioned above that there were competitions in the recitation of poetry, and 'marks' given for the recital of such-and-such a poetic classic, of which it is clear the *Gododdin* was one. There are signs that the use of writing, learned from the Latin tradition of the Celtic church, was beginning to be applied in a very sketchy manner to the recording of native texts as early as the end of the sixth century in Ireland, though it probably did not begin to become common there before the eighth; but there is no reason at all to suppose that in Wales the writing of either poetry or prose literary texts in the vernacular had really begun at all before the end of the eighth century at earliest.

The poems in the Book of Aneirin are not the only heroic eulogies and elegies addressed to characters of the late sixth or early seventh centuries. To argue from this that they are therefore genuine would be fallacious unless these can be themselves proved genuine; and, as with the *Gododdin*, this can neither be proved nor disproved – it can only be made probable. Among the very heterogeneous

---

[1] Adherents of the Milman Parry theory would do well to note that there is not the slightest evidence for so-called 'improvisation' in the well-known history of the oral poetic tradition in the Celtic literatures.

compositions attributed to Taliesin, Sir Ifor Williams picked out a dozen heroic eulogies very like the *gorchanau*, mostly addressed to Urien of Rheged and therefore a little earlier than the *Gododdin* if genuine, for the authenticity of which, following Morris-Jones,[1] he made out a good case.[2] Nor are these the only such eulogies whose metre, type of alliteration, style, language, and vocabulary are strongly reminiscent of the *Gododdin* and date ostensibly from this period. We have already discussed a fragment of one from Strathclyde apparently composed in 642. An even more notable one is the panegyric[3] on Cadwallon, king of North Wales, the ally of the Anglian king Penda of Mercia against the Northumbrians, who was killed in 634 near Hexham by Oswald king of Bernicia. It is in a metre, style, and language of the same kind as we see in the *Gododdin*, and obviously belongs to the same bardic tradition. There are actually verbal echoes of the *Gododdin* like the line-beginning *caeawc cynhorawc*, 'wearing a brooch, in the front rank', which introduces the chain of verses 2, 4, and 5 in the A. text. It mentions Edwin, king of Deira and Bernicia 617–33, as leader of the men of Bernicia, and there is a reference to 'the muster for the burning of York', which must have been part of the devastation of Northumbria by Cadwallon and Penda, told of by Bede, which followed the killing of Edwin at Hatfield Chase in 633 (which dates the poem 633–4 if contemporary with the events, as Sir Ifor thinks it is). It is important to note, incidentally, that it speaks of 'the grief for Catraeth, great and famous'; that is to say that the composer of 633–4 knew of the fame of the battle of Catraeth, and presumably the *Gododdin* itself, a generation before, and quoted it in connection with the exploits of the Welsh under Cadwallon against the Northumbrians. Lastly, another heroic

---

[1] See his *Taliesin*, volume XXVIII of Cymm. (in English).
[2] In his CT. (in Welsh).
[3] Edited by Williams, BBCS. VII, 23 ff. (in Welsh).

lay of the first half of the seventh century is the elegy on
Cynddylan,[1] a Welsh king of the middle Severn valley
and the opposite Welsh border country. The same remarks
about metre, style, and language apply to this, *vis-à-vis* the
Gododdin, as to the Cadwallon poem. The Welsh tradition
of a somewhat later period says he fought at the battle of
Maserfield in 642 in which Oswald, king of Northumbria,
was killed by Penda, and the elegy itself speaks of him as
taking part in an attack on Lichfield in Mercia. Here
again we seem to have the voice of authenticity; and
although these poems do not at all prove the genuineness
of the *Gododdin* they do at least provide very striking
parallels, not to be lightly disregarded.

It has been shown above that the older B. text of the
Gododdin derives from a lost MS. probably of the ninth or
tenth centuries; that the text of that MS. was *already* corrupted by scribal miscopyings implying the existence of a
still older written source; and that behind *that*, it is clear
there had been a period of oral recitation during which
the arrangement of the verses had become badly dis-
ordered, stanzas had been duplicated, or confused in part
with each other, interpolations had crept in, and so on; all
arguing a considerable length of time during which the
text had tended to go to pieces owing to poor memory and
faulty recitation. One should add that in the A. text likewise the similar oral corruptions, independent of those in
B., show that it too had had its period of non-written
transmission, separately from B. Hence if we suppose that
the first written copy of the *Gododdin* belonged to, say, the
early ninth century, which is reasonable, we must suppose
a space of at least a century or two before that to allow for
these corruptions, which, considering the nature of the
professional training of the Celtic bard, is a moderate
estimate. But this takes us back close to the time of Catraeth

---

[1] Edited by Sir Ifor Williams, BBCS. VI, 134 ff., and CLH., pp.
50 ff. (in Welsh).

itself. The writer wishes to record, then, his firm conviction that the poems were indeed put together quite soon after the battle, and that the battle itself may fairly be dated 'about 600' (with a bias for a slightly earlier date than this convenient round-figure one; see the Introduction § 2).

But with a qualification. The poems were composed orally and handed on orally for two centuries or more. During that process a considerable degree of modernisation of language would inevitably occur; some obsolete words and archaic grammatical forms and constructions no longer intelligible would be replaced by neologisms, and quite likely some newer metrical features might put in an appearance; not to mention interpolations and spurious alterations like the evidently secondary calculation whereby the force that went to Catraeth numbered 363 and three escaped, not one. In the course of such drastic modifications it might be expected that the original metre would suffer; and in fact something of this sort is needed to account for the very distinct irregularities in the numbers of the syllables in the lines which characterise many of the verses all through the poem. But this is quite natural, granting the history as just sketched. In this sense, then, the *Gododdin* and its *gorchanau* are the work of Aneirin about 600, but only in this sense.

If the poems were composed in Edinburgh, how did they get to Wales, particularly since the collapse of the independent kingdom of Gododdin before the middle of the seventh century would have brought about the collapse of its bardic organisation as well, after which it is incredible that they could have been handed down there? Now, the work of Aneirin is by no means the only body of sixth to seventh century Northern literary tradition which reached Wales. The considerable remains of the story of Urien, the legends centred round the battle of Arfderydd, a number of genealogies of Northern princes, and other matter still more fragmentary, are further instances.[1] Indeed the Heroic Age of the British people in the early post-Roman period is to a large extent a Cumbric rather than a Welsh one. It is difficult, of course, to discuss such a question when so little is known about this dark period, but perhaps one might venture to suggest that the Celtic literary institutions flourished more, in the conditions of Roman Britain, in the North than they did in Wales precisely because Wales was part of Roman Britain and for most of the time the North was not. In Wales we have a firm Roman military rule controlling and no doubt allowing little independence to a number of highland chiefs, whereas north of Hadrian's Wall the typical Celtic political organisation, with its warrior aristocracy and its bardic profession, could continue quite unrestrained. This is not to say, of course, that Wales lacked these things – quite the contrary, as there is clear evidence to show – but that in the circumstances it is likely that heroic poetry and saga would prosper less in the south than they would in the North, with its wholly independent princes and the opportunity for constant warfare (a necessity for heroic literature but more or less denied to the Welsh under Rome) between Britons and Picts, and Romans too. Now, during the course of the sixth and seventh centuries the whole British North came into the power of Northumbria, with the very important exception of Strathclyde; which, with its capital at Dumbarton, its religious centre at Glasgow, and its heartland the valley of the Clyde, but reaching probably from upper Loch Lomond and Cunningham to Peebles and the source of the Tweed, held on to its independence for some three and a half centuries after the rest of southern Scotland had fallen to Northumbria. It is here, at the court of the kings of Strathclyde, that the stories of the Northern Heroic Age must have flourished. The men of Strathclyde had their own bardic poetry and

---

[1] See also Mrs Bromwich in SEBH., pp. 121 ff.

heroic tales, of course; we should know this must be so *a priori*, but by a miraculous chance an actual fragment of it survives to prove it in the form of the interpolated verse about Dyfnwal Frych discussed above. It would be from Strathclyde, surely, that all this Northern literary material eventually reached Wales.

That literary contact was maintained between Wales and the North long after the two were separated politically by the Northumbrian and Mercian expansions of the seventh century is known from a number of sources.[1] For instance there is reason to believe that Nennius in Wales early in the ninth century made use of a Latin historical document on the relations between Britons and Northumbrians put together from older sources somewhere in the North (perhaps Glasgow?) at the very beginning of that century.[2] Again, when the Welsh sages were gathering genealogies, somewhere between 954 and 988,[3] to illustrate the claim of Ywain son of Hywel Dda to be king of much of Wales, and drew to a large extent on an older collection probably dating from the reign of his ancestor Rhodri Mawr (844–77),[4] the latter material provided them with several northern pedigrees, and above all with that of the kings of Strathclyde down to one Rhun who came to the throne there in 872. This suggests that the literary men of Wales had a particular interest in the North in the ninth century, and we may perhaps suppose that a text of the *Gododdin* came south about this time, along with all the rest. The poem was *known* in the south before that, doubtless orally, as we see from the eulogy on Cadwallon, but

[1] It would be naive to suppose that such contacts must have come to an end once this separation had taken place. For one thing, as Mrs Chadwick has often very rightly emphasised, the Irish Sea was a bridge, not a barrier, at this period.

[2] See the writer's article in *Celt and Saxon* (edited by N. K. Chadwick, Cambridge, 1963), pp. 20 ff.

[3] Probably soon after 954.

[4] On all this see H. M. and N. K. Chadwick in GL. I, 149 ff. and 273 ff.; and cf. Lloyd, HW. I, 159, 345.

possibly it now reached Wales for the first time in manuscript. The reason for thinking this is as follows. We have
seen that the verse about the Strathclyde victory at
Strathcarron in 642 was probably interpolated in written
form on the opening page of a manuscript of the B. text.
It is likely that this would happen in Strathclyde rather
than in Wales, and if so, that there must have been a
manuscript of the *Gododdin* in circulation there; and if the
the Welsh 'learned' and written, rather than bardic and
oral, interest in the North was responsible for bringing it
south, it is likely to have happened between the end of the
eighth century and the end of the ninth – just the period
already proposed on other grounds for the oldest written
text. Sir Ifor Williams thought that the fact that the North
Welsh dynasties claimed descent from a prince of Gododdin, Cunedda, was responsible for the interest taken in
Aneirin and his work in North Wales.[1] This may perhaps
be true, and would account for its oral currency or at least
fame there at a distinctly earlier date, about 634, within
living memory of the battle of Catraeth; but it is not likely
to have existed in MS. form so early. If the above history
of the text is correct, it should be observed that the extensive oral corruption which lies behind the written version
would have taken place in Strathclyde, not in Wales.

It is a question how well-known the *Gododdin* really was
in Wales. The rubric at the end of the Gorchan of Cynfelyn,
and the other evidence mentioned in § 15 above, would
appear to suggest that it was a universally familiar classic,
particularly the rubric which, to paraphrase it, states un-
equivocally that no bard who hoped to win the prize at
the poetic competition ought to think of competing unless
he could recite the *Gododdin*. But if so, it is a curious fact

[1] CA., p. xix. It should be noted that he believed it must have come
straight from Gododdin to North Wales, and soon after the battle,
because 'it would have had little hope of lasting long in south-eastern
Scotland'. Evidently he did not consider the possibility of the inter-
mediary of Strathclyde.

that only one manuscript of it has survived, and one whose textual tradition is so corrupt. A constant recitation by professionals who prided themselves on their exact knowledge of this 'classic' should have kept the text in a much better state of preservation. Setting aside the rubric, which is in any case suspect for its absurd and typically pedantic notion about the size of the 'mark' at the competition, as well as for its mention of Taliesin and the multiplied numbers of the army of Gododdin and its survivors, it looks rather as if the poem was not in actual fact at all familiar and in common currency by, say, the twelfth century. Rather, it would suit the evidence better if we could envisage an ancient classic widely known by name, reputation, and general nature, fragments of which circulated orally and were recited in a corrupt form, but which was not really any longer well known as a whole, and possibly never had been in Wales as distinct from Strathclyde. If so, the rubric would be the work of someone inventing a situation as he thought it ought to be and not as it actually was.

Addendum. According to the Welsh 'Chronicle of the Princes', in the year 890 the King of N. Wales, son of the Rhodri mentioned on p. 65, settled a body of Strathclyde exiles in parts of the east of his kingdom after they had helped him expel the English who occupied them. This would have been a favourable opportunity for Northern poems, traditions, and MSS. to reach Wales.

Appendix

A number of historical, geographical, and other points need a rather fuller discussion than could be given them in the body of the Introduction. These are as follows.

1. Gododdin and Manaw Gododdin

The manuscripts of Ptolemy differ over the exact reading of the tribe name, but the best, on purely internal textual evidence alone, is ὠταδινοι, which is also the nearest to the *Wotādīnī demanded by the form *Gododdin*. The missing *w-* cannot easily be explained by the fact that Greek had no *w*-sound, since it regularly uses *ου* for this in rendering non-Greek names, and Ptolemy follows this custom elsewhere. Williams' explanation[1] that a blank may have been left in his exemplar for decorated initial capitals to be filled in later, and that the scribe neglected this, may be correct. The *ω* instead of *ο* is easily explained when we remember that Ptolemy was using Latin sources, in which the name would appear simply as *Uotadini*. In any case the identification cannot be doubted. The name was known, quite naturally, to the Gaelic Scots of Dál Riada (Argyll), and through them, to the Irish. With them, it took a form spelt *Fotudán* in early Irish, where *t* means *d* and *d* means ð,[2] which is likewise the phonologically

---

[1] CA., p. xviii.
[2] That is, the *th* in English 'this'.

correct development if we grant two premises: (1) the name was borrowed by the Scots from the Britons some-where about the year 600, by which time it had already become *Wodoðin* in Cumbric, and the Gaelic syncope of unstressed internal vowels had by now ceased to have effect; and (2) the Cumbric *-in* suffix may have been taken for the Gaelic diminutive suffix *-ín*, which was a good deal rarer than the alternative *-án*, which therefore replaced it by 'suffix substitution'.[1] The Gaelic colony of Argyll was beginning to expand eastwards in the late sixth century, and it would be quite natural that this name should be taken over about the time in question.

In Nennius' *Historia Brittonum*, chapter 62, he tells how Cunedda and his sons came to Wales, as already noticed above, from the north, from the region called 'Manau Guotodin'; this is Old Welsh, and would be 'Manaw Gododdin' in Modern Welsh. This has led to an extra-ordinary misunderstanding, which has become so en-grained of recent years in the works of Dark Age historians[2] and others, that like so many other fallacies about the Celtic evidence on the Dark Ages, it will probably go on appearing for many years. It consists in identifying Manaw Gododdin and Gododdin, which are really two quite distinct things. In its most extreme form, R. G. Colling-wood, in a passage which has probably been responsible for a good deal of the popularity of this error, identifying Manaw Gododdin with the whole country of Ptolemy's *Otadinoi*, says that it is 'round Berwick-on-Tweed'.[3] Many other scholars, however, are under the impression that Lothian, including Edinburgh, is really what is meant.

[1] See on this *Celtica* III, 165 f., and the *Scottish Historical Review*, XXXVI, 129, 134; 'the conspicuous peak of Fodudhán' is very likely North Berwick Law.

[2] Including very strangely H. M. Chadwick (as edited by N. K. Chadwick) in ES., passim, e.g. p. 4, 'seems to have been situated be-tween the Tyne and the Forth'.

[3] RBES., p. 289.

Even Sir Ifor Williams, who marks 'Manau' and 'Guotodin' correctly on his map in CA., p. xvii,[1] and protests
against Berwick-on-Tweed, speaks of it as 'near North
Berwick and Edinburgh', though he perhaps mentions
North Berwick purely to contrast it with Berwick-on-
Tweed; seen from Caernarvonshire on a small scale map,
there would probably not be much difference between
Manaw and the neighbourhood of North Berwick. It is
unfortunate that either Berwick was ever introduced into
the discussion, as both are irrelevant. In fact it has long
been recognised that Manaw Gododdin is not a unitary
name like New Zealand, in which the first element qualifies
the second, but that the name proper is *Manaw*, and that
in this phrase *Gododdin* is added as a qualifier, rather like
Asia Minor. Gododdin here is syntactically genitive, and
the meaning is literally 'Manaw of Gododdin', that is,
'Manaw *in* Gododdin', and the purpose of this qualification
is to distinguish it from the other Manaw known to the
Welsh and Cumbrians in the Dark Ages, namely the Isle
of Man.[2] It may perhaps surprise some of those who talk
glibly about 'Manaw Gododdin' in relation to, say, East
Lothian, to hear that this phrase occurs nowhere but in
the passage from Nennius mentioned above and in the
note in the Old Welsh Genealogies giving the names of
Cunedda and his sons, obviously related to Nennius, and
rests on this sole authority. Far from being the normal
name of the kingdom of Gododdin, 'Manaw Gododdin' is
quite unknown elsewhere; and most significantly of all, is
never found in the poems of Aneirin, who calls the kingdom by its proper name, Gododdin, throughout.

If so, where and what is Manaw? The Old Irish equiva-
lent is *Manu*, genitive *Manonn* or *Manann*; and leaving

[1] Cf. the Ordnance Survey *Map of Britain in the Dark Ages*, 2nd ed.
(1966).
[2] Rhys and Skene speak of another Manaw 'in the north'—but
significantly do not identify it!

aside a battle in the year 582 or 583 on the grounds that this was probably fought in Man rather than Manaw, we have another, certainly in Manaw, in 711, when the Annals of Ulster give 'a slaughter of the Picts in the plain of Manu (*in campo Manonn*) by the Saxons'. Now, the Anglo-Saxon Chronicle has the same battle, but with a quite different and independent geographical identification – *betwix Hæfe & Cære*; that is, between the rivers Avon and Carron, which flow into the Firth of Forth on either side of Falkirk, the former rising near Slamannan in the hills to the south of Falkirk and the latter in the range sw. of Stirling. On the south side of the Firth the 'plain' in question is narrow and hemmed in by hills, but it extends from Grangemouth just east of Falkirk north-west to Stirling and round the head of the Firth, south of the Ochils, and eastwards past Alloa and Clackmannan to Kincardine opposite Grangemouth.[1] It was pointed out long ago that Slamannan (*Sliabh Manann*, 'the Moor of Manu') and Clackmannan (*Clach Manann*, 'the Stone of Manu', referring to a celebrated rock now protected by a railing in the

---

[1] I should like to add that Nennius in his chapter 65, having spoken in the previous chapter of an expedition by Penda in 654 to the 'city which is called Iudeu', then continues that Oswy then returned (*reddidit*) all the riches which he had with him in the town *usque in manau Pendae*, according to the best MS. (H), though the reading of MS. K, *manu*, is generally adopted. The whole passage about Oswy and Penda is rather obscure. In *Celt and Saxon*, p. 35, I suggested one should read *in manum Pendae*; but there is something to be said for accepting the reading of H, as some have done (e.g. Anderson, AES. I, 15 f.; it is, after all, the *lectio difficilior* as well as having the better authority), in which case *usque in Manau* would be a misplaced gloss on *usque ad urbem quae vocatur Iudeu* in chapter 64, perhaps due to the second *usque*, and Iudeu would be in Manaw. This suits very well the view (see *Celt and Saxon*, p. 36 f.) that Iudeu is Stirling; without Stirling, a Manaw on both sides of the Firth would not have been viable, and whatever we think of the corrupt passage in Nennius there seems little doubt that Stirling must have been its capital. It would be just within, and would defend, its western borders. The 'sea of Iuddew' in verse B.27 of the *Gododdin* is in any case undoubtedly the Firth of Forth.

main street) contain this name; and therefore inferred that Manu-Manaw was a small province round the head of the Firth of Forth. But there is not the slightest evidence that it ever extended any further, and indeed to talk about *the* plain of Manaw if the name included all Lothian as well, which has several separate 'plains', would be absurd, and utterly ludicrous if it included the whole Gododdin country to the Tyne and beyond.

Scottish historians in modern times have always been well aware of this. The best and clearest discussion is that by W. J. Watson in his CPNS. in 1926,[1] who examines the place-name evidence and says 'this is agreed to have been a district about the head of the Firth of Forth', and that it was 'the district round the head of the Firth of Forth whose name remains in Slamannan and Clackmannan'. One may mention also Skene, *Celtic Scotland*, I, 131, who makes Manaw reach east from the Carron to the Pentlands, and ibid., p. 254, west from the Pentlands to the Roman [Antonine] Wall, which limits it too much in the north-west since he had not realised the significance of Clackmannan.[2] Further, A. O. Anderson, AES. I, 12, n. 1, 'Manau (East Stirlingshire);' ibid., p. 213, n. 3, 'Manau, i.e. Clackmannanshire, with an extension to the south of the Forth, as far as Slamannan'; 234 n., 'the Carse of Falkirk was the southern part of the ancient Manau'. Note the same author's *Adomnan's Life of Columba* (London, 1961), p. 42, 'Manau, which included Clackmannanshire and extended to the south of the Roman Wall, as far as Slamannan'; and Mrs Bromwich in SEBH., p. 154, 'Manau Guotodin which lay near the head of the Firth of

[1] CPNS., pp. 103 f., 128, 130 f.
[2] There is absolutely nothing to show that it reached so far east as the Pentlands, though they would form a good eastern boundary (because Manaw had a *campus* it does not follow, of course, that it was all plain). At any rate if one tries to stretch it any further east, beyond the Pentlands, one comes up against the barrier that a quite different *campus* starts here.

Forth'. One may compare Lloyd, HW. (1st ed., 1911), I, 118, 'on the northern border of the country of the Votadini, where Slamannan in Stirlingshire still keeps the name alive'; and Morris-Jones, Cymm. XXVIII (1918), 74, 'Manaw, generally identified with the country round Slamannan, south of the Forth'. It seems that the wide extension attributed to Manaw, and the vague idea that it is the *same* as Gododdin, is a comparatively recent growth; and the above authorities have been stressed here because I want to make it clear that I am not proposing a novel heresy but emphasising a well-established fact which has got lost sight of by scholars who are not specialists in Celtic history and philology.

'Manaw of Gododdin', then, was a small province on the far north-western boundaries of Gododdin, but probably made important by the possession of the key border fortress of Stirling. The notion that it was a large region, co-terminous with Gododdin, may perhaps have been supported in the minds of some by the idea that Cunedda, summoned to North Wales to expel the Irish, must necessarily have brought with him a vast army and must have been a powerful king. But as to this, we know nothing. Remembering other great conquests by small, determined forces such as the little band of Norman adventurers who won southern Italy, one sees absolutely no reason why Cunedda and his sons should not have been famous professional warriors with a fairly small company, invited (or, if one theory is correct, transferred by Roman agency) to Wales to drive out the Irish occupants by organising and leading local resistance. He may have been simply a noble – there is nothing to show he was king of Manaw, still less of course of Gododdin – whose emigration was not thought likely to weaken seriously the province from which he came, or the north-western defences of Gododdin. In any case the whole story has suspect features; not to mention the fact that the theory of 'a deliberate piece of

Roman policy', beloved of some historians, runs up against another one – that the Irish themselves had been settled in Wales in the first place as *foederati* as 'a deliberate piece of Roman policy'. And in any event the migration of Cunedda is now regarded as having taken place so late that it is not credible it was due to Imperial organisation.[1] It looks a good deal more like the sort of thing we seem to see in reverse in the *Gododdin*, men of Gwynedd coming north to help their kinsmen against an alien enemy; though very likely on a larger scale.

It may be added that if the Stirling region was the far north-western boundary, somewhere not far from Catterick may have been the far south-eastern. Ptolemy shows the Wotadini reaching south east to the neighbourhood of the Wear, and Catterick itself may have been thought of as not far outside its borders. At any rate, a passage in A.73 which says of a hero killed at Catraeth that 'the borderland of Gododdin is his grave' may reasonably be taken to imply this. But of course considerable parts of the maritime strip of Gododdin must have been in Bernician hands by about 600.

2. Eidyn

There have been doubts in the past whether the *d* here means *d* as in 'wading' or *th* as in 'bathing', and whether the vowel in the second syllable is properly *y* or *i*. That the vowel was *y* was finally proved by Morris-Jones, who also showed at length that the *d* meant *d*;[2] compare also the treatment of the name by Watson in CPNS., p. 340 f.[3] However, the older idea that it meant *th* was revived by Sir Ifor in CA., pp. xxxvi ff., though very hesitatingly. The

[1] Cf. p. 21, n. 1, above.

[2] Cymm. XXVIII, 77 ff.

[3] It is unfortunate that Williams seems to ignore Watson all through CA., since some wrong identifications, some of which may have a long life, would otherwise have been avoided. Thus, the Irish *Dún Monaid* is of course not Edinburgh (CA., p. xxxviii); see CPNS., pp. 391 ff., particularly 394.

evidence for this last view is exceedingly weak and is entirely outweighed by that for *d*, which means that apart from a slight difference in the initial diphthong the name rhymes with English *wadin'* and not with *bathin'*;[1] and authorities on Welsh writing recently seem to accept that this is so.[2]

The name Eidyn occurs by itself in B.6, 21, 28, 34, and A.17, 18, and 76. Some have thought that Eidyn was not a 'city' but a district, around Edinburgh, but none of the above examples gives any clear guidance here except A.17, where 'the hall of Eidyn' makes it perfectly plain that Mynyddog's capital is meant, not a region. Apart from this, the name is more clearly defined as Din Eidyn in B.19, as already described above; exactly *Edin-burgh*. Caer Eidyn does not in fact occur,[3] but only *Eidyn gaer*, in the Gorchan of Cynfelyn,[4] which would best be rendered 'Eidyn the fortified town', with lower-case letters, just as *Eidyn ysgor* in A.13 is 'Eidyn the stronghold'; *esgor Eidin* in the Gorchan of Maeldderw[5] is 'the stronghold Eidyn'. In other words, the *name* is Eidyn or Din Eidyn,[6] and the others are descriptive phrases. One may compare the early Welsh names for Dumbarton, capital of Strathclyde. In Old Welsh this was *Al(t) Clut*, 'The Rock of the Clyde', but other early sources call it also *din Al Clud, caer Al Clut, din Clut*, and *caer Glut*, and in Latin *arx Alt Clut*, which are likewise descriptive phrases rather than the true name.

The chief reason for supposing that Eidyn was a district,

---

[1] See AS., pp. 39 ff., where the case is argued in detail. To the evidence adduced for *th* on p. 40 there, one should add that in *Minit Eidin* in the Black Book of Carmarthen, p. 95, l. 7, the contrast between *t* meaning *th*, as it normally does in this MS., and the *d* which normally means *d* in it, strengthens the case.

[2] E.g., A. O. H. Jarman in BIK., pp. 196, 198, etc.

[3] I was wrong over this in AS., p. 38.

[4] CA., l. 1385.

[5] CA., l. 1441.

[6] Din Eidyn also occurs in the Book of Taliesin, p. 29, l. 18 (ed. J. G. Evans).

not a town, is the fact that Carriden, the site of the Roman fortlet of Velunia at the eastern end of the Antonine Wall on the Forth about three miles north of Linlithgow, has been taken to be Caer Eidyn, and with Din Eidyn being Edinburgh this has been held to imply that Eidyn was a province comprising these two places. Various scholars have thought this, including Sir Ifor Williams (CA., p. xxxviii). A capitula interpolated by one Cormac, presumably an Irishman, in a thirteenth century copy of Gildas *De Excidio Britanniae* speaks of *Kaireden, civitas antiquissima*, at the east end of the Antonine Wall; *c.* 1148, Carriden appears as *Karreden*, in 1336 as *Karedene*, and in 1335–6 as *Carden*.[1] But first, a name Caer Eidyn does not exist; secondly, Carriden is stressed on the first syllable, and was actually pronounced in the eighteenth century Cárrin,[2] which makes it impossible it can come from Caer Eidyn, as Watson shows;[3] third, the Roman name of the little fort was Velunia, and it is very unlikely it would have been re-baptised with a new name like 'the Fortified Town in Eidyn' when it lay in ruins and its real name was forgotten; fourth, the scribe may very probably have had *Karreden* in his exemplar, and either misread the *rr* as *ir*, which is very easy, or took the name for a Caer one and very likely knew of Eidyn as a *civitas antiquissima* – if he lived in far-away Ireland the fifteen miles between Carriden and Edinburgh Castle would mean nothing to him.[4] Lastly, no one seems to have noticed that if Eidyn were a region it would be unexpected that a town in it should be called Din Eidyn or Caer Eidyn. What would these mean? 'The Fort of the country of Eidyn' and 'The Fortified Town of the country of Eidyn'? Such would be at least

[1] CPNS., 369 f.; A. Macdonald, *The Place-Names of West Lothian* (Edinburgh, 1941), p. 25 f.
[2] The modern spelling is due to the influence of the traditional form, as so often happens.
[3] Loc. cit.
[4] Cf. Macdonald, loc. cit.; and AS., p. 39.

anomalous, though perhaps not entirely unparalleled, in
the Brittonic onomastic system.[1] Moreover, to have *both* at
once would be absurd; *Din* and *Caer* mean very much the
same thing, so that 'Din Eidyn' and 'Caer Eidyn' would
not be sufficiently distinguished. *Din X* and *Caer X* really
mean respectively 'The Fort X' and 'The Fortified Town
X' or (on the analogy of Housman's 'Uricon the city') 'X
the Fort' and 'X the Fortified Town'; they can hardly
mean respectively 'the Fort' and 'the Fortified Town' of a
district called Eidyn. In view of all the above, the theory
must be abandoned, and with it, the idea that Carriden is
Caer Eidyn. There *was* no *Caer Eidyn*; there was *Din Eidyn*
and there may have been *caer Eidyn* with lower-case *c-*,
just as there was *ysgorva Eidyn*. *Eidyn* and *Din Eidyn* are
parallel exactly to 'London' and 'London Town', and *caer
Eidyn* to 'the town of London', with capital T in the former
and small *t* in the latter.

3. Bannog

A range of hills somewhere in the north of Britain, called
in Old Welsh *Bannauc* and in Middle Welsh *Bannawc*,
which would be Bannog in Modern Welsh, sometimes
appears as an important boundary in early sources, though
it is clear that the authors were vague about its where-
abouts, hence a corresponding vagueness among some
modern scholars. Since the best known mountain barrier
in Scotland is the Grampians it has been identified with
this by Sir Ifor Williams[2] in CLH., p. 156 f., though if he
had known Watson's CPNS. he would hardly have done so.
In the Latin *Life of St Cadog*, put together about the year
1100, the Welsh St Cadog comes to a certain town *citra
montem Bannauc* (that is, 'to the south' of it), 'which is said
to be in the middle of Albania', where in digging the

---

[1] Names like Dinllaen or Dinorwig are really not relevant, as the
second elements here are tribal names.

[2] And following him, by Mrs Bromwich in TYP., p. 278.

foundations for a monastery he finds a gigantic bone, and raises its owner from the dead. The giant tells him that his name was Cau of '*Pritdin*' and that he was formerly king *ultra montem Bannauc*, but that he came raiding to this region and was killed with his army by the king of the country.[1] Now the church of Cambuslang in Strathclyde, just SE of Glasgow, is dedicated to St Cadog, and Bishop Forbes and W. F. Skene took the range to be the Cathkin hills in Car*munnock* parish west of Cambuslang; but this makes no sense, since these hills do not divide anything of any significance from anything else likely to have earned them a name as an important boundary; cf. Williams, loc. cit. Besides, Cau came from 'Pritdin', which is a slightly anomalous spelling for Old Welsh *Pritin*, Middle Welsh *Prydyn*, 'Pictland'. Caw of Pictland is known in early Welsh tradition; he figures as a chief of the North with a large number of sons some of whom became saints, notably St Gildas, whose eleventh-century *Life* says he was born in Strathclyde and that his father was *Caunus*, a simple scribal error for *Cauuus = Cawus*. On him see further TYP., p. 302. Gildas would presumably have been thought of as fathered by Caw after he had been resuscitated, or at least after he had come to Strathclyde from Pictland. The fact that Caw is of Pictland shows that the Cathkin hills make no sense, and so does the location of Cadog's monastery 'this side (i.e. south) of the mountain of Bannauc'. The clue was pointed out by Watson as early as 1926;[2] Bannog is the hills in which the *Bannock* Burn rises, as already remarked in the Introduction, § 1; strategically one of the most significant mountain barriers in Scotland and forming the southern boundary of Pictland in the west.

[1] See A. W. Wade-Evans, *Vitae Sanctorum Britanniae* (Cardiff, 1944), pp. 82 ff. By the time of the Life of St Cadog *Albania* was a term for the whole of modern Scotland.

[2] CPNS., p. 195; compare *Antiquity*, XXIX (1955), 81.

4. Deira and Bernicia

Both these names are probably Celtic in origin; that is to say, the Anglian settlers of both regions adopted the tribal names of the British inhabitants already there, a common enough phenomenon with immigrant and conquering peoples. Both *Deira* and *Bernicia*, which are Bede's forms, are Latinised feminines singular, like *Britannia*. The Anglo-Saxon tribal name is respectively *Dere* and *Bernice* (*Bærnice, Beornice*). The oldest contemporary source in Welsh is Nennius' *Historia Brittonum*, chapters 61 and 63, in which the former is invariably *Deur* and the latter in the two best MSS. *Berneich* twice and *Birneich* once.

In the *Gododdin* there are two quite distinct forms for the men of Deira. One is the same as Nennius', spelt *Deor* in B.28, where it seems certain that Deira is meant. The difficulty here is that there was another word identical in form but meaning 'bold', and it is not altogether clear which it is in the other cases in the *Gododdin*. In B.14, 15, and 16 the phrase *deor daen*, and in A.62 *dewr daen*, occurs, which is quite probably 'scatterer of the men of Deira' but might be 'bold scatterer' or 'scatterer of bold men' (cf. CA., p. 254); all these four instances are closely connected, as variants or repetitions. In A.50, CA., l. 623, Williams would take the *dy wr* of the MS., ostensibly 'thy man', as another example; but this is more than doubtful. The other form in the *Gododdin* is *Deivyr* (spelling for *Deivr*), which is found in A.5 and 18 and certainly means Deira. In later medieval Welsh *Deivr, Deifr* is still common both in the precise sense of the northern English and in a looser sense of the (English) enemy in general;[1] but *Dewr* seems not to have survived, no doubt because of the awkward clash with *dewr* 'bold', though perhaps some cases in poetry apparently meaning the latter may really conceal the former.

[1] See G., sv.

These forms are full of problems. *Deur-Dewr* is the oldest and is quite definitely established, but its relation to *Deira*, and to *Deivr*, also well-established in Welsh if probably later,[1] is wholly obscure, and even that of *Deivr* to *Deira* is by no means clear.[2] As to the etymology, Rhys derived the name hesitatingly from **dubro-* 'water',[3] so that Deira would mean 'the land of the waters', but though this was widely accepted it raises great difficulties and ought to be abandoned. See the discussion of the point in LHEB., p. 419 f., and add to the authorities there cited Förster in *Archiv für das Studium der neueren Sprachen*, CXLVI, 133, and *Englische Studien*, LVI, 224 (but Förster's treatment, though it is interesting, is quite unsatisfactory; for one thing, the developments he postulates, particularly *vr* giving *r*, could scarcely have taken place as early as the time when the Angles first settled in Deira and borrowed the name. Moreover not only Nennius but also the *Gododdin* show that *Deur, Dewr, Deor* cannot be spellings for *Dyvr*).

The name Bernicia is almost equally difficult. It has been generally thought that it is a derivative of that seen in the name of the British tribe of the Brigantes, placed by Ptolemy in Yorkshire, southern Durham south of the Wotadini, Cumberland, Westmorland, and Lancashire; but such an explanation raises such problems of phonology that it would be best to give it up altogether, as is suggested in LHEB., pp. 701 ff. One may add to the arguments given there, the striking fact that the land of the Brigantes ends precisely where that of the Bernicians begins, that there is no overlap at all, and that the old identification is therefore still more severely weakened.

[1] *Deivyr* in our MS. can easily be a scribal modernisation.
[2] A British **Dabria* or **Dobria* would account for *Deivr* and might for *Deira*, but will not explain *Deur*, which even a **Debra* would scarcely do satisfactorily; and the etymology of such forms remains obscure.
[3] In the forms *Debria* or *Dobria*, neither of which are acceptable; see J. Rhys, *Celtic Britain* (SPCK., 2nd ed., 1884), p. 291.

5. Saeson

As we have seen, early Welsh, including the poems in
the Book of Aneirin, called the English in general *Lloegrwys*, a name of unknown origin; the Saxons *Saeson*; and
the Angles *Eingl* (used later sometimes of the English); the
last two respectively from *Saxones* and *Angli*. But it has
often been remarked that *Saeson* was frequently applied to
English regions where the inhabitants were not Saxons
but Angles; and this is true of the *Gododdin* itself in A.13
and 51, where the Anglian people of Northumbria are
called by this name. Are we to suppose that the Welsh
were so careless of ethnographic accuracy that they did
not trouble to distinguish between them? The explanation
is rather different. Saeson is a name borrowed from Latin
during the Roman period, as its form shows, and for the
Romans the Germanic pirates and mercenaries against
whom they had to guard by building the chain of forts of
the *litus Saxonicum*, the *Saxon* Shore, were *Saxones*, not
Angli. The clue is to be found in some words of Myres' in
RBES., p. 343: 'The latter term [Saxones] came to embrace
in the common parlance of those within the empire the
whole group of north German peoples whose homes lay
along the coast-line beyond the Franks. . . . To the
frightened provincial the precise ethnology of those who
looted his villa was a matter of indifference – Angles or
Jutes, they were all Saxons to him. . . . The Celtic
peoples, following in this respect the usage of their Latin-
speaking ancestors, continued for centuries to label all the
Teutonic inhabitants of Britain as Saxons. . . . They
[the Angles] too, when they learnt in the seventh century
to write Latin, adopted at times the convention customary
in that idiom, to the denial of their own tribal origins'.
P. 347 f., 'The word Saxon . . . had widened its scope to include all the peoples between the Elbe and the Rhine, and
eventually became . . . little more than a term of abuse'.

6. Catraeth

In CA. pp. xxxii ff. Sir Ifor discusses at length whether the Catraeth of the poems can be Catterick, philologically speaking. There is no doubt at all that it can. The English *Catterick* is a secondary form with suffix-substitution, and the primary Anglo-Saxon is *Cetreht* in the Anglo-Saxon version of Bede. This would come quite naturally from a Cumbric **Catracht*.[1] The forms given in Bede's original Latin are *Cataracta* and, in the ablative, *Cataractone*, the second implying a nominative *Cataracto*; earlier, Romano-British, documents confirm the *-on-* suffix, but there is no doubt that whatever the ultimate origin of the name, it had become *Cataracta*[2] in late Latin, as evidenced by Bede, and this is the direct source of the Welsh and Anglo-Saxon forms. A Late British **Cadarachta*, which is how *Cataracta* would develop in that language, would become **Cadracht* or **Catracht* by the second half of the sixth century, when the men of Deira were probably approaching and beginning to settle in this region, and **Catracht* would give Anglo-Saxon *Cetreht* and later Welsh and Cumbric *Catraeth* quite regularly. Sir Ifor made some difficulty about the *-tr-* instead of the expected *-dr-* in Welsh, but the group *-d'r-* arising by syncope in Late British can perfectly well undergo provection to *-tr-* as an alternative form,[3] even without having to postulate *-d'rr-*, and the *-tr-* is confirmed by the English forms. There is no doubt, therefore, that the traditional identification of Catraeth with Catterick is unobjectionable philologically.

[1] On all this see Förster, FT., p. 119.
[2] The name may always have referred to the falls of the Swale at Richmond, transferred to the river, and thence (as often happened with British names, e.g. *Deva* 'the Dee' becoming the name of Roman Chester) to the town on it; or if its origin is different, it became confused later with Latin *cataracta*. See the discussion by Ifor Williams, loc. cit., and LHEB., pp. 409, n. 1, and 564.
[3] See Morris-Jones, *A Welsh Grammar* (Oxford, 1930), p. 183 f.

That the identification is also probable historically is
suggested by the significance of Catterick as a Northumbrian 'capital' at the time, continuing its Roman importance, and as a strategic point in the northern road system;
and also as the place where a blow aimed at two allied
kingdoms would be most likely to succeed, by splitting
them. The fact that it is far from Edinburgh and a long
way south of the northernmost Bernician settlements is
seen to be no objection when one compares the deep
penetrations into England made by Scottish plundering
bands in the course of the mediaeval and later Border raids,
as well as by invading armies; particularly if Mynyddog's
party took the western, Carlisle, route (which incidentally
points straight at Catterick). 'Catterick' occurs also in
'Catterick Moss' in Co. Durham, a name not recorded
before 1311, but to suggest that this is Catraeth, on the
ground that it is nearer Edinburgh, would face four objec-
tions: (1) The difference in distance is not great enough to
have any real significance; (2) unlike Catterick, the place
is not situated strategically on the road-system from the
north; (3) unlike Catterick, it can have had no political
importance; and (4) Catter*ick* is not a natural development of *Catracht* but has undergone an anomalous suffix-
substitution, and it is not credible that such a substitution
could have happened twice by coincidence. In Catterick
Moss the name is therefore of some different origin, unless
indeed we agree with Ekwall (Oxford Dictionary of
English Place-Names) that it is simply taken from the
Yorkshire Catterick – much later than our period, of
course.

7. Cavalry, and Romanisation

The question of the employment of cavalry by the men of
Gododdin has been canvassed above and answered in the
affirmative. Since the use of cavalry as an organised
military tactic was unknown in general in Dark Age

Britain but was familiar to the Romans under the Empire, it has been supposed that this is evidence for the survival of Romanisation of the British peoples on the outer border of the Empire in the north. That some degree of Romanisation must be reckoned with is certain. Like their compatriots in Wales, these people quite often bore Roman names; they were Christians, an aspect of Romanisation; they wore coats of mail, called by a name borrowed from *lorica*.[1] They fought in properly drawn up ranks and perhaps 'squares', and one might even venture to ask whether the occurrence once or twice in the *Gododdin* of phrases like 'he marshalled a bright shining array . . . he was in charge of a hundred men' (B.13) could refer to some sort of officer descended from the Roman centurion.

The evidence therefore that the cavalry of Gododdin are ultimately of Roman origin seems plausible. But the purpose of this note is to sound a caution. It has become a favourite dogma among some writers that the British peoples in the Dark Ages had a great military organisation like a sort of Horse Guards or Dragoons, and that in particular this is true of King Arthur. It was probably the romantic and eloquent account of the supposed activities of Collingwood's 'Artorius, *comes Britanniarum*',[2] which has been responsible for this; and the fact has been lost sight of that there is not the slightest real evidence that Arthur, if he ever existed, had anything whatever to do with cavalry. The arguments offered to support this, such as that his supposed 'battles' are widespread, his force was therefore 'mobile', and he was therefore a cavalry commander; or that the Roman *comes Britanniarum* commanded cavalry and therefore Arthur did, are tendentious, and the second is circular. The idea is unconsciously derived in the first place, no doubt, from the much later medieval stories of

---

[1] But the early Anglo-Saxons did so too; the word, *byrne*, occurs for instance several times in Beowulf.

[2] RBES., pp. 320 ff.

Arthur's 'knights'; it is conveniently forgotten that
Arthur's armoured knights are figments of the romantic
imagination, and that Geoffrey of Monmouth, the earliest
source of anything of the kind and a notorious journalistic
forger, spoke of Arthur's men as *equites*, 'knights', because
as a Norman author he naturally could not conceive of
high-class warriors as anything else. A look at the older,
traditional Welsh, picture of Arthur's men as seen in the
story *Culhwch and Olwen* and elsewhere including Nennius'
Mirabilia, tells a very different story, for those sources at
any rate (and Geoffrey had no other). The matter is
further discussed by the present writer in chapter 1 of
R. S. Loomis' Arthurian encyclopaedia 'Arthurian Literature in the Middle Ages' (Oxford, 1959); see particularly
p. 8 f., and on Arthur's 'battles', pp. 4–8. But no doubt we
shall see characters in Welsh Dark Age tradition claimed
as 'Roman cavalry officers' for a long time to come.

8. Recent Criticisms of the Date *c.* 600

Since Sir Ifor Williams' ably argued defence of the
genuineness of the poems – and he seems to have thought
of a text actually written by Aneirin and handed on mainly
in writing, which is not credible – only two voices have
been raised in serious published criticism so far as I know.
It appears now to be generally agreed that the parent
British language had evolved into the earliest form of
what can be called Welsh (and Cumbric) about the middle
of the sixth century, and the question is whether a poem
like the *Gododdin* could have been composed in the new
stage of the language so soon afterwards, little more than
half a century later. The two most important linguistic
developments in the evolution from British to be borne in
mind here are that all British words (except of course
monosyllables) lost their final syllables and those com-
pounded of two elements joined by a composition vowel
lost this vowel, a phenomenon apparently completed by

the middle of the sixth century;[1] and that a little later, words which were now of three or more syllables might lose further an interior unstressed syllable, though they did not necessarily always do so.[2] This means that all British words of more than one syllable were now at least a syllable shorter in the earliest Welsh, and many were two syllables shorter. Consequently, a British poem composed in syllabic metre say in the late fifth century would have collapsed in metrical anarchy if 'translated' into the language of the late sixth century.

Principal Thomas Parry has raised some interesting doubts about the above problem.[3] He asks whether by the end of the sixth century the new language could have 'evolved and established such a highly developed metrical system as is displayed in these poems'. The present writer attempted a brief answer in *The Modern Language Review*, LVII (1962), 605. To expand what was said there, we must consider what is involved. The basic features of the system are syllabic length of lines, stanzaic construction, rhyme, and alliteration. But there is nothing at all about the last three which would be affected by the change from British to Welsh. The late Latin popular and hymn metres had both rhyme and stanzaic construction, and these were duly carried over to their descendants in the Romance languages, a far bigger transference than from British to Welsh; nor is there any reason why alliteration should not also have been so transferred if Latin had had it. As for the syllabic length of the lines, the final and unstressed internal syllables of British had completely gone by about the middle of the sixth century, and some fifty years had passed since then before the battle of Catraeth. We ought not to suppose that a change like the (in any case gradual) disappearance of these syllables would suddenly strike the

[1] See LHEB., § 182.
[2] Op. cit., § 197.
[3] *The Oxford Book of Welsh Verse* (Oxford, 1962), p. 538.

poets of Britain dumb, and for an extended period. In fact it is clear that there can have been no unbridged gap in the history of Celtic poetry in Britain, since it carries on the Celtic traditions shared with Ireland; and it would be strange if there were. The poets must have continued to compose, but now in the *dolce stil nuovo*, and it is not for nothing that Taliesin and Aneirin and their contemporaries were called the *Cynfeirdd*, the 'first' or 'earliest' poets (of the new Welsh and Cumbric language). They would simply accommodate the language, with its now shorter words, to the older syllabic metre, which would be perfectly easily done, though it is true that since British was stressed on the penultimate syllable and the new Welsh on the ultimate this would give lines of a different stress pattern. But the position of stress is irrelevant to syllabic poetry, and this would therefore be of no consequence. The 'highly developed metrical system' spoken of by Principal Parry is really not so highly developed that all these things would be at all impossible.

The other criticism mentioned above is to be found in *The Celtic Realms*, by Myles Dillon and Nora Chadwick (London, 1967), pp. 216 ff. Professor Dillon thinks that British could not have evolved so rapidly that by the end of the sixth century the language could have reached the stage of development we see in the Book of Aneirin. He would seem to admit that these poems cannot, in any case, be later than the ninth century, but will not allow that such a stage could have been reached three centuries earlier. In his opinion they were composed in the ninth century on traditional themes, and he compares the Middle Irish poems put in the mouth of St Columba who lived centuries before. He calls the reasoning of Morris-Jones and Ifor Williams in favour of the genuineness of the Taliesin and Aneirin poems 'incomplete', though as he does not discuss any of it, or attack the theory on any grounds *other* than linguistic, this is not a wholly convincing line of argument. The theory that the *Gododdin* is a late 'forgery' is dealt with elsewhere in this book, but it is right to say that the poems attributed to St Columba are an entirely different affair. They are not heroic poetry praising a number of people by name who would have been long forgotten if Dillon's view were correct, but are religious lyrics invented in later times as part of the glorification of one of the most famous saints of the Celtic church at all periods. It would have been more to the point to compare the *Amra Choluim Chille*, an Irish poem on Columba now generally agreed to have been composed in his lifetime, late in the sixth century, with the Archaic Irish prose of the beginning of the eighth century. Allowing for the fact that the *Amra* is in a very ancient type of metre preserving what were probably already some syntactical archaisms, the difference is not so very great here either. The same sort of thing applies to the sixth century Leinster poems mentioned by Dillon himself on his p. 226.

To say that the Welsh language of the end of the sixth century could not have been so closely like that of the ninth is an *a priori* argument without substance. In the first place, we do not really *know* at all what it was like at that time, so far as syntax and idiom, and to some extent morphology, are concerned; but in the second, the present writer seems to have shown in L H E B., or at any rate without anyone contradicting it, that phonologically there was no drastic difference between the Welsh of about 600 and that of about 800 or 900 – so drastic, that is, that a poem composed at about the former date could not perfectly easily be modernised into ninth century dress without seriously altering it. Languages are apt to be subject to very violent and relatively sudden linguistic evolutions, 'earthquakes' as it were, as happened to British in the fifth to sixth centuries, after which they may remain with very little if any fundamental change for centuries; one might well bear in mind, here, the history of the Irish language for some centuries after the 'earthquake' of the Middle Irish period. One can say with confidence that there is no reason at all why the quite newly-established, post-'earthquake' neo-Brittonic dialects of Primitive Welsh and Primitive Cumbric should have been wildly unlike what they were two centuries later. After all, we must remember that no one is arguing – or at any rate the present writer is not arguing, for it would be quite untenable – that the B. text, still less the A. text, of the *Gododdin* is exactly what Aneirin composed. We must not think of him as sitting down and *writing* a poem, which has come down to us through an unbroken series of manuscript copies, little altered in any linguistic essentials. On the contrary, as has been made plain above, both versions have behind them a long history of oral transmission, during which the language was inevitably continually modernised by reciters; so that if the B. text *were* linguistically no earlier than the ninth century there would be nothing surprising in that. There is no claim made here that the Book of Aneirin is the *ipsissima verba* of Aneirin as they stand; only that it is a modernised and corrupted version of them which nevertheless preserves the essential character and contents, and broadly speaking the wording, of his work.

A priori arguments apart, Dillon mentions two – and only two – features of the language of the *Gododdin* which he thinks cannot be so old, and so near to the parent British, as about 600; the fact that adjectives qualifying plural nouns, and verbs governed by plural nouns, may both be constructed singular, as later in Middle Welsh. But this too is *a priori*. Do we really know that this was impossible in Primitive Welsh-Cumbric about 600 – or in the parent Late British either, for that matter? To say that it was, is nothing but a feeling, a guess; and in any case we are not arguing that Aneirin himself used the singular in such cases, but only that the text has come down to us in that form. It is true that e.g. in the two lines CA., l. 1136 f. (B.9), *trychan meirch godrud a gryssyws ganthud*, the singular adjective *godrud* is proved by rhyme and the singular verb *gryssyws* would make the line a syllable too long if turned into the plural. But what would the plural of *godrud* be? It probably comes from a British singular *wotrōtos; do we know that the plural of this was not *wotrōtī – in which case the Welsh plural would be *godrud* too? As to the verb, there are two answers. First, to read the plural, *a gryssyassant*, would admittedly make one syllable too many; but the irregularity of the *Gododdin* about line-length has already been pointed out, and in this verse of eight lines of five-syllable metre there is already one which is a syllable too short, so that another syllable too long would be nothing surprising. Indeed, Williams specifically points out in CA. p. lxxiii that the five-syllable metre may in general vary with six syllables or with four,[1] so that this need not be regarded as an irregularity at all. And secondly, the difficulty can perfectly easily be removed by emending the second line to the more archaic *cryssyassant ganthud*, also plural; compare CA., l. 611, *byssed brych briwant barr* and other such.[2] One must conclude, in the light of all that has been said, that there is no real substance in the argument put forward in *The Celtic Realms*.

[1] A.1 is a good example of this.

[2] On the question of agreement of verbs and adjectives with plural nouns see Simon Evans in BBCS. XVI, 76 ff. In the famous *Gwyr a aeth Gatraeth* of A.8, 9, 10, 11, and 12 (CA., ll. 68, 74, 84, 90, 97) the singular verb is however proved by rhyme; but this is in the A. text.

PART II

The Poems

The Poems

Note on the Translation

In previous editions and translations of the *Gododdin* the
A. text has always been given first because it comes first in
the manuscript. Sir Ifor himself did this, but wherever an
A. verse had a variant in B., or within itself, he printed the
variant immediately after the other verse. This was convenient for purposes of comparison, but unless one has
handy – and can read – the diplomatic edition of Gwen-
ogfryn Evans, or some other one which is in the same
order as the manuscript, it is exceedingly confusing if the
reader wants to follow the poem as it really is. I have
therefore given the two texts with their verses in the exact
order of the Book of Aneirin, with a cross-reference at the
head of each to the variants if any. With one difference,
however; that the B. version comes first here instead of
second, because as it stands it is some centuries older and
is on the whole more original, though it is true that the A.
text evidently preserves the order of the verses distinctly
better. To find in *Canu Aneirin* the text of any of the
verses as rendered here the reader need only consult the
reference at the beginning of each; and to discover, when
using *Canu Aneirin*, where in this book – or in the manuscript – the relevant verse appears he may use the Con-
cordance given below on p. 159.

The principle on which the summary version and discussion offered here has been constructed is mentioned briefly in the Preface. Some verses are translated in full, others in part, and others summarised only, depending on how intelligible they really are and how interesting. Where the A. and B. versions differ in wording I have not substituted the one for the other even when it is fairly clearly superior, so long as it makes sense in the context, though I have done so if one is quite obviously wrong; we are dealing primarily with oral variation, which gives one much less right to act as editor in such matters than written variation does. All translations appear within inverted commas; omissions are indicated by rows of dots,[1] and where a translation is given without such dots it may be taken that this is a complete verse. When a word is queried it implies that this meaning is really quite doubtful, but perhaps at least worth giving; but it must not be assumed that all words not queried are necessarily certain, by any means. The translation is intended to be fairly literal, but there may be a certain degree of paraphrase where it is desirable to prevent too literal a rendering from being too ugly, or unclear; e.g. where in B.22 'he was not base where he was seen' is rendered 'his behaviour was not base to see'. There are a good many cases in the poems of the 'historic present', and these are rendered as the past tense, as also is the imperfect unless there is some special point in emphasising 'used to'. Here and there, words and brief phrases not in the original have been added, shown by square brackets, where necessary to elucidate the meaning. Part of the difficulty in early Welsh bardic verse lies in the fact that its nouns and adjectives have no inflections except for the plural (and then only partly in the adjective), and therefore, unlike the situation in for instance Latin, it is

---

[1] A row of dots in translations in the Introduction above means simply that, in a passage translated, something not relevant to the discussion has been left out.

not always entirely clear which word belongs with which.

I have entered into few discussions of readings and meanings, apart from some brief notes which are intended for the non-specialist reader, to throw light on the translation where necessary (and a few references to notes on the text published since CA.). There would be no point in anything else, since Welsh scholars will understand perfectly well, in the light of Williams' edition, why such-and-such a translation is given and what it implies. They will know, of course, that his method was to canvass every possible interpretation of a difficult word and to give all those with any pretensions to plausibility, including some with rather little, and then often to leave the conclusion open, or to indicate his own preference only very hesitatingly. Unless he is to enter himself into long disquisitions without interest to most readers of a book like this, a translator is therefore obliged, where he has no new suggestion of his own to offer, to make a choice of what seems to him the most likely meaning, without justifying it. This may be a question of individual opinion; and though the instances where I have differed from the great Welsh scholar's choice – or apparent choice – are not many, others will realise that I have done this because I think a different alternative suits the context better, or for similar reasons. I should add that where I have followed Williams' emendations of the text (and he did not emend drastically or often) this is also done silently; Welsh scholars will understand this and others will not be interested.

The Translation

The Archaic Text B

B.1 = CA. lxxix B

See the variant A.78, which is close to this. This is the interpolated verse on Dyfnwal Frych and the Battle of Strathcarron in the year 642 discussed in the Introduction, § 14. The picture in B. seems to be that at dawn the army of Dyfnwal Frych attacked and fired a town on a hilly headland, and the inhabitants came out to defend it, perhaps in two detachments. The headland might be the ridge on which Falkirk stands. 'They had arisen', etc.; Williams (see p. 47 n. 3 for the reference) would emend here and in A.78 *ac wyr Neithon* 'with the grandson of Neithon', and takes B.'s *ry godessyn* for a different verb, meaning 'they were angry', and would read the same in A.78. This would make 'them' the men of Dál Riada, not those of Strathclyde. But this makes the line a syllable short in both verses, and it seems very plausible that we should read *a gwyr wyr Nwyth(y)on ry godessyn* in A.78, 'and the men of the grandson of Nwython had arisen'; and in B.1, *o eir wyr Nwython ry godessyn*, as is done here; leaving the question open which reading is original. The whole verse runs, with the one emendation and two readings from the A. version:

'I saw an array, they came from the headland, and splendidly they bore themselves around the conflagration. I saw two [groups], they had come down swiftly from their town, they had arisen at the word of the grandson of Nwython. I saw great sturdy men, they came with the dawn; and the head of Dyfnwal Frych, ravens gnawed it.'

B.2 = CA. lv B

See the variant A.52. Here the reciter of the poem stands up in the hall and prefaces his recitation of the poem with this verse, on which see § 14 of the Introduction; also § 6.

'*Gododdin,* I make my claim boldly on your behalf in the presence of the throng in the court, with the lay of the son of Dwywai of high courage – may it be manifest in the one place that it vanquishes [all others]. Since the courteous one, the rampart of battle, was slain, since the earth covered Aneirin, poetry and the men of Gododdin are now parted.'

B.3 = CA. li C

See the variants B.24 and A.48. A difficult verse on one Grugyn, who is called 'a slab of rock in cleared land', that is, a great standing stone in an open space? There is a reference to 'fair play before the borderland of Gododdin', and to a troop coming from across the sea in a ship, 'the bodyguard from Din Dywyd'; and the verse ends 'The shield of Grugyn, it was broken-fronted before the field of battle'. Din Dywyd is unknown (identification with Dundee is impossible, see CPNS., p. 220), and it is not perfectly clear who is coming 'from across the sea', but apparently the men of Grugyn; who would very likely have been from Pictland if so.

B.4 = CA. lxxxvii B

See the variant A.86. The hero is Gorthyn son of Urfai of the race of Cilydd (A.86 Garthwys son of Erfai of the race of Clyd), from Rhufoniog in Gwynedd (North Wales), from

the banks of the river Aled; see the Introduction, § 8. The
verse begins by describing him as 'A destructive flood in
every lowland' and 'the defender of Rhufoniog', and says
that 'his battle-horses and his bloodstained armour were
seen around the Aled . . .' It continues:

'. . . He was stern in contest, he slew with a spear, a
hundred men bore away his harsh warning from battle,
[yet] he provided song at the New Year feast. Any lady
or maiden or well-born man could approach the son of
Urfai, could approach the proud boar; and since he was
the son of a rightful king, lord of the men of Gwynedd,
of the blood of Cilydd the gentle, before the cheek of the
generous, thoughtful, sage man was buried in the earth
his gifts and his fame brought visiting throngs; and it is
sad that Gorthyn the tall from the borderland of Rhufoniog is in the grave.'

'His harsh warning' is presumably wounds inflicted by him,
and this is contrasted with his liberality as a host and his
approachability.

B.5 = CA. xliii B

See the variant A.40. This verse forms a 'chain' with (or is
perhaps a loose variant of) B.6, just as A.40 does with A.41,
variant of B.6. The opening in all four is unfortunately
obscure (beginning in B.5 'For the very wretched . . . ,
for the smiling land and the waste . . .'), and it is not clear
who is being praised, since four or five people are mentioned in the four verses; but certainly Morien is one, and
the story of the hero tackling the wolf bare-handed seems
to apply to him rather than to Bradwen. B.5 names Morien,
as fighting 'the heathen' (the English; emending from
B.6), 'and the Gaels and the Picts', and the verse ends with
a mention of 'the stiff red corpse of Bradwen' and of
'Gwenabwy son of Gwen'. On Bradwen and Morien see
also B.7.

B.6. = CA. xliv B

See B.5, and the variant A.41. This verse begins 'For the very wretched feast . . . , [for] the heavy, compact, very waste land . . .' Morien is spoken of as 'looking at Eidyn'; and it ends:

'. . . His gauntleted hand was raised against the heathen and the Gaels and the Picts; he who may drag the mane of a wolf without a spear in his hand must always have bold fierceness under his mantle. I will sing that Morien would not have died, [nor] the just (?) Gwenabwy son of Gwen.'

B.7 = CA. liv B

See the variant A.51. The verse is in honour of one Addonwy, but Bradwen reappears for comparison, and in A.51 both Bradwen and Morien, so that B.7 probably belongs with B.5 and 6 though it hardly forms a 'chain' with them; and if so, A.51 is misplaced. B.7 begins 'Good was the fortune, Addonwy, Addonwy, which you had promised me, that what Bradwen would do you would do; you would slay, you would burn. You did not last on the wing or the van. . . .' This refers to the warrior's 'boast' before battle; cf. the Introduction, § 12.

B.8 = CA. xc

This forms a 'chain' with B.9; there is no variant.

'Three hundred men hastened forth, wearing gold torques, defending the land – and there was slaughter. Though they were slain they slew, and they shall be honoured till the end of the world; and of all us kinsmen who went, alas, but for one man none escaped.'

B.9 = CA. xci

There is no variant. 'Three hounds' means 'three heroes'.

'Three hundred men, wearing gold torques, battle-loving, performing feats (?); three hundred proud men, united, fully armed; three hundred spirited horses hastened out with them; three hounds and three hundred; alas, they did not come back.'

B.10 = CA. xcii

There is no variant. The whole verse runs:

'Bold in battle, mighty (?) when hard-pressed; in conflict there was no truce that he would make, in the day of wrath he would not shirk the fight. Bleiddig son of Eli was a wild boar for fierceness; he drank off wine from brimming glass vessels; and on the day of combat he would do feats of arms, riding his white steed. Before he died he left behind him bloodstained corpses.'

B.11 = CA. xxiii B

The first part of this verse appears corrupt, and the first short-line is missing; the second part is a loose variant of the second part of A.23, but the two verses deal with two different people. For fuller discussion see A.23. The second part of B.11 is:

'. . . He used to make men prostrate and women widows, before his death. It was Bleiddgi's son's right to form the [battle-] pen in the presence of the spears.'

B.12 = CA. xx B

See the variant A.20, which is part of a chain with A.19 and therefore in its right place there. The hero's name in A.20 is Breichior.

'. . . When everyone else fled you attacked. If the blood of all those you killed were wine you would have (?) plenty for three years and four, [and yet] you would diminish it vastly for your steward. May you attain the land of Heaven because you did not flee. Breichiol the stubborn was world-famed.'

B.13 = CA. xxii B

This verse belongs with A.22, though it is not a variant of it; rather it makes a chain with it linked at the ends but not at the beginnings. The 'son of Cian' is evidently the same person as the one mentioned in A.9, and coming from 'beyond Bannog' would make him a Pict, see the Appendix no. 3; his name is Llif in B.13 but Llifiau in A.22, which is adopted as the better reading here. The whole verse is:

'When he attacked in the borderland his fame was renowned, he deserved [his] wine, the man wearing a gold torque. He marshalled a bright shining array, the bold one; he was in charge of a hundred men, the noble warrior of renowned spirit, the foreign horseman, the young only son of Cian from beyond Bannog. The men of Gododdin do not tell of anyone more harsh than Llifiau when he was on the field of battle.'

B.14 = CA. lxiii D

The relation of B.14, 15, 16 and 36 and A.62 is a complicated affair, and there is considerable confusion. All but B.36 start with a long-line beginning 'the anchor' and ending 'the forefront of the army' (B.16 has prefixed to this a corrupt long-line which probably does not belong); and all but B.16 end with three lines beginning 'truly are you called', with incremental repetition, B.14 and 36 praising Tudfwlch and B.15 and A.62 praising Merin son of Madiain (Madiaith in B.15). It looks as if B.36 does not really belong at all, but has had this three-line ending added fortuitously; that B.14 and 15 really stand in incremental relation to each other and A.62 is a variant of B.15; but that B.14 and A.62 have quite different middles between the above opening and closing phrases and B.15 has lost this middle altogether. The phrase translated 'the scatterer of the men of Deira' could be 'the bold scatterer'; see the Appendix no. 4.

'The anchor, the scatterer of the men of Deira, the serpent with the terrible sting, the immovable rock in the forefront of the army; vigour in reinforcement, violence in great straits, the meritorious lord with force of spears. For your loyal deeds truly are you called the ruler, the prince, the rampart of every compatriot; Tudfwlch the forceful in slaughter, the barrier of the fortress.'

B.15 = CA. lxiii B

See the note on B.14. *Madyeith* here is emended *Madyein* from A.62. The line in parenthesis after the first 'called' is obviously a mere repetition of the previous one by error.

'The anchor, the scatterer of the men of Deira, the serpent with the terrible sting in the forefront of the army. For your loyal deeds truly are you called – for your loyal deeds rightly are you called – the ruler, the prince, the rampart of every nation. Merin son of Madiain, in a fortunate hour you were born.'

B.16 = CA. lxiii C

See the note on B.14. A 'following water' presumably means a flood bearing down on someone trying to escape it. Williams treats *garth Merin* as a place-name, but B.15 and A.62 show that Merin is the hero of the verse, and I take *garth* ('enclosure') here in the sense of 'battle-square'.

'The bright flood, the grey wolf, the terrible following water; the anchor, the scatterer of the men of Deira, the immovable rock in the forefront of the army. There were bloodstained troops of horses and men before the men of Gododdin, the swift hounds baying them; the division mustering, the defence . . . in front of the battle-square of Merin.'

B.17 = CA. xciii

On an unnamed hero. 'He would not kneel to anyone'

presumably means would not beg for quarter. On holly-
wood spears and guarding the ford see the Introduction § 9,
and on 'the honoured portion' § 12.

'With his shield suffering blows, he would not kneel to
anyone, he used to foster love of honour (?); terrible
. . . horses in the van of battle. In strife they showered
holly-wood spears. . . . When my comrade was struck
he struck others, there was no insult he would put up
with. Steady in guarding the ford, he was glad when he
bore off the honoured portion in the palace.'

B.18 = CA. xxvi B

See the variant A.26, which is twice the length of B.18.
'True' at the beginning is accepting the reading of A.26;
B.18 has 'false' here. There is nothing to show whether the
Tudlew of B.18 or the Cadlew of A.26 is more original; but
in either case the warrior praised is Marchlew. The verse is:

'It was true what Tudlew said to you, that no one's
horses could overtake Marchlew. Though he were not
reared by the gates . . . his swordstroke was mighty
in his [battle-]station (?). Plentifully he used to scatter
his ash spears from the five fingers of his hand, from his
slender dappled steaming [horse].'

B.19 = CA. xciv

There is no variant. The hero is Gwaednerth.

'The protection of Heaven, the dwelling-place in the
longed for land [be his]. Woe to us for grief and unceas-
ing sorrow, when the nobles came from the region of
Din Eidyn, the picked men of every prudent lordship.
As they strove with the mongrel hosts of England there
were nine score around each one, around [each] mail-
clad [warrior]; a multitude of horses and armour and
silken clothing. Gwaednerth defended his rights in
battle.'

B.20 = CA. lxi B

See the close variant A.60, and compare A.58 and 59 which make a chain with it.

'From the retinue of Mynyddog they hastened forth; in a shining array they fed together round the wine-vessel. My heart has become full of grief for the feast of Mynyddog, I have lost too many of my true kinsmen. Out of three hundred wearing gold torques who hastened to Catraeth, alas, none escaped but for one man.'

B.21 = CA. xcv

There is no variant. 'Like swans' means either as white, or as graceful, as swans. 'Had gone rolling', lit., 'had turned over'. 'Who would not flee', see the note on A.2.

'The retinue of Gododdin on rough-maned horses like swans, with their harness drawn tight, and attacking the troop in the van of the host, defending the woods and the mead of Eidyn. Through Mynyddog's policy shields had gone rolling and blades had fallen upon white cheeks; they loved . . . attack, they did not suffer reproach, the men who would not flee.'

B.22 = CA. xcvi

There is no variant. On Elfed see the Introduction § 1.

'I drank off mead at one draught on my journey, wine-fed before Catraeth. When he struck with blades, steadfastly and eagerly, his behaviour was not base to see, he was no wretched wraith in giving support. Madog of Elfed was a destructive bearer of a shield.'

B.23 = CA. xcvii

There is no variant. For Aeron the poem has Arfon, the country in Caernarvonshire opposite Anglesey; this is improbable, see the Introduction § 5. On Aeron = *Ayr*shire see § 1. The whole verse is:

'When he came to the fight he was not one who would be likely to escape with his life, the avenger of Aeron, wearing gold ornaments, he attacked, the opponent among the Britons. Cynon's horses were spirited.'

B.24 = CA. li B

See the variants B.3 and A.48, particularly the note on B.3. This verse on Grugyn begins 'A slab of rock in cleared country, in cleared country a hill, [on the] borderland of Gododdin . . .'; there is the same reference to the troop from overseas and to 'a . . . motley band from Din Dywyd . . .'; and it ends '. . . the shield of Grugyn, it was broken-fronted before the bull of battle' (i.e. Grugyn himself).

B.25 = CA. xlv B

See the variants B.35 and A.42. The verse, on Cynhafal, is in part difficult and corrupt. It ends '. . . No one who is alive can tell of the adventures of the chief, about him whose figure was of brilliant mould. No one who is alive tells that Cynhafal was not an ally on the day of battle(?).'

B.26 = CA. xcviii

The verse, on Nai son of Nwython, begins with four rather difficult lines, and then continues:

'. . . He slew a great host to win reputation, the son of Nwython slew a hundred princes wearing gold torques so that he might be celebrated. It was better when he went with a hundred men to Catraeth. He was a man reared and nourished on wine, of generous heart; he was a blessed, active man, he was wearer of a broad mail-coat, he was fierce, he was rash, on the back of his horse. No man put on armour for battle – vigorous were his spear and his shield and his sword and his knife – who would be better than Nai son of Nwython.'

B.27 = CA. xcix

There is no variant. On the 'sea of Iuddew', which is the
Firth of Forth, see the Introduction § 1, and the long foot-
note in the Appendix no. 1. Bubon would therefore either
be a Pict or would be from the northern part of Manaw
across the Forth. The whole verse is:

> '[From] over the sea of Iuddew, very bold in battle, three
> times worse in ferocity than a fierce lion, Bubon be-
> haved with mighty wrath.'

B.28 = CA. c

There is no variant; the hero praised is Urfai son of Golistan. Whether he was father of the Gorthyn son of Urfai
from N. Wales praised in B.4 is very doubtful, not only
because the A. version of B.4 reads Erfai, and because there
is nothing in B.28 to suggest a Welsh background, and
because he is called a 'lord of Eidyn', but also because it
does suggest a young man whose father had little influence,
and who was therefore hardly likely to be accompanied to
Catraeth by a son of military age. The whole verse runs:

> 'It was usual [for him] to defend Gododdin on a spirited
> [horse] in the forefront of battle . . .; usual that he should
> be swift on the track of the deer; usual that he attacked
> in front of the household troop of Deira; usual for the
> son of Golistan (though his father was no great lord) that
> what he said was listened to; usual were shields broken
> on behalf of Mynyddog; [usual] a red spear before that
> lord of Eidyn, Urfai'.

B.29 = CA. lxix B

See the quite close variant A.68. The scene at the beginning
is the jubilation of the men in Mynyddog's hall before
setting off. The point of the week's diary is unclear, but it
can hardly mean that the battle lasted from Friday to
Monday, as it appears to at first sight, if the tactic was a

sudden shock attack by a tiny force of cavalry. More likely the whole thing is anticipatory till Monday ('corpses were counted up' would mean 'boasted of in anticipation', and so on). The (doubtful) reading of A.68 for Sunday need only mean at most that the battle began on Sunday and was finished on Monday. The whole verse is translated here, but the last eleven words have dropped out in the B. text and are supplied here from A.68; q.v. On the last sentence see the note on A.2.

'[Even] the court-officers could not bear the [shouts of] praise in the hall, at the contention of the bodyguard, a contention which was suppressed (?), like a blazing fire at its kindling. On Tuesday they put on their fine armour, on Wednesday their common purpose was bitter, on Thursday envoys were pledged, on Friday corpses were counted up, on Saturday their united deeds were unrestrained, on Sunday red blades were distributed, on Monday streams of blood were seen up to the knees. The men of Gododdin tell that when they returned to Madog's tent after the long fatigue [of battle] there came no more than one man out of a hundred.'

B.30 = CA. xl

Compare the chain A.37, 38, and 39; also (except 39) on Eithinyn. This short verse begins with virtually the same line as A.39, 'He attacked in [battle-]stress for the cattle-herds of the East . . .', and the poet says '. . . I honour him, . . . with the greatest courage in return for mead, a fine fortunate daring veteran, Eithinyn the renowned son of Boddw. . . .'

B.31 = CA. xli

There is no variant.

'The exalted men went from us, they were fed on wine and mead. Because of the feast of Mynyddog I have become sorrowful, for the loss of the harsh warrior.

Shields resounded like the thunder of heaven before the onslaught of Eithinyn.'

B.32 = CA. lxxi B

This verse on an un-named warrior forms a chain with B.33; see its variant A.70, where the name is given as Gwrhafal.

'Arising early in the morning, when warriors rush forwards in the army, following from outpost to outpost, he charged the foremost before a hundred men. He was as greedy for corpses as for drinking mead or wine. It was thus eagerly he struck the enemy, the . . . fierce overbearing lord.'

B.33 = CA. lxx B

See B.32, and B.33's variant A.69.

'Arising early in the morn, in conflict with a chief before the boundary, he was bitter (?) when standing at bay in the van of the battle. A beloved friend . . . , he was courteous and tenacious, he was grave, he was fierce. . . .'

B.34 = CA. ci

There is no variant. Edar appears to have repulsed some previous attack on Edinburgh. 'His gifts to the enemy' etc. means that he was generous to captives after the feast celebrating victory? Or, he boasted much, at the feast before the battle, of the 'gifts' (i.e. spears etc.), that he would 'give' the enemy?

'His blades were seen in the army, as he withstood the stern enemy; at the clatter of his shield men fled, they fled before Eidyn, the hill . . .; there did not come back as much of it as a hand could grip; there was wax on it and . . . He was stubborn, with his shield hacked small; when he was thrust at he thrust, he did not [need to] give a second blow; he struck, he was struck. His gifts to the enemy were frequent after the feast; he was venomous . . . ; and before he was buried under the sods of the earth Edar deserved to drink his mead.'

B.35 = CA. xlv C

See the variants B.25 (and the notes on this) and A.42. Like these others, this short verse on Cynhafal is mostly obscure and corrupt. It ends '. . . The *Gododdin* does not tell that Cynhafal was not a supporter on the day of battle (?)'.

B.36 = CA. lxiii E

See the note on B.14, on the series of more or less related verses of which this is one. Calling Tudfwlch 'the herb-garden of the war-band' perhaps means that he provided or organised their feeding, but one suspects it is a looser and more general metaphor than that.

'[With] bloodstained blades covering the ground, the hero red in his fury – the man-slaying champion – was wont to be joyful like a wolf at his post, the wolf of the army, the herb-garden of the war-band, a champion slaying; before he was blinded [in death] he was no weakling. For your loyal actions truly are you called the ruler, the helmsman, the rampart of every compatriot, Tudfwlch the forceful in slaughter, the barrier of the fortress.'

B.37 = CA. lxxv B

See the partial variant A.74. The hero is un-named. For the untranslated words *bot ero* here after 'land' one should perhaps substitute *Pobdelo*; compare A.74.

'He met with violence, the black slayer of a host of brigands, he was not without repute nor an outlaw, he was not a . . . bitter-sweet drinking-companion; grey horses neighed (?) under his protection; he was no profit to the land . . .; the bull of battle did not retreat the width of a single acre, his purpose was stubborn. . . .'

B.38 = CA. cii

There is no variant. This is the verse with the famous reference to 'Arthur', who is treated here as a paragon that no hero can quite equal. There is of course no guarantee that it was in the original *Gododdin*, but if it was, and if the poem was composed about the year 600, it is by far the oldest known reference to King Arthur and dates from a time when people who remembered him would still be alive. Arthur was the great national hero of the entire British people, from Scotland to Brittany, and there is therefore no logic whatever in the idea that this reference can be used to support the theory that he was a Northern leader.[1] The last words probably refer to the fact that shields were often made of alder wood, and mean that Gwawrddur alone was as good as a whole 'shield wall'.

> 'He stabbed over three hundred of the finest, he slew both the centre and the wings, he behaved worthily in the forefront of the most generous army; he gave out presents from his herd of horses in the winter. He glutted (?) black ravens on the rampart of the stronghold, though he was no Arthur. . . . In the van, Gwawrddur was a palisade of alder (?).'

B.39 = CA. lxvi B

B.39, 40, and the fragmentary 42 are a chain beginning 'A most fitting song' (B.41 is wrongly inserted in this chain, to which it does not belong), and A.63–67 are a chain beginning 'A fitting song' and obviously related to the one in B. The relationship is complicated, but A. is evidently fuller and preserves the original better. To put it briefly, B.39 is repeated by the close variant A.65 (but the first line of B.39 belongs to B.42, from which it is taken); B.40 is repeated by the close variant A.63; and when B.42 was complete it would probably have had its close variant in

[1] TYP. p. 275.

A.66. 'The barrier of Aeron' is Cynon son of Clydno, the subject of the verse; see the Introduction § 5. The eagles praised him because he provided them with carrion in battle. 'Better by far' strikes one as odd, but the thought is really 'there was none better, and *he* was better by far'.

'A most fitting song of a skilful company; and before the barrier of Aeron had passed away the beaks of eagles praised his hand. In frenzy he made food for carrion birds, for the sake of Mynyddog the horseman of hosts; he set his side against the spears of the enemy. Before Catraeth the wearers of gold torques were active, they pierced, they slew those who withstood (?); the cubs of violence were far from their land. Rare in battle was a man from among the Britons of Gododdin better by far than Cynon.'

B.40 = CA. lxiv B

See the note on B.39. 'The trees of battle' is a kenning for 'warriors'. The last sentence seems to mean that he took communion before going to Catraeth, but was killed and therefore never received his 'pay'.

'A most fitting song of a company was got. Our warriors had made embroilment around Catraeth; a trampling of bloodstained chequered cloth was trodden down, the trees of battle were trampled in retribution for earning their mead; with corpses it was settled (?). Cibno does not tell, after the uproar of battle, that he got his dues though he took communion.'

B.41 = CA. ciii

This verse is wrongly interpolated into the chain B.39, 40, and 42, presumably because it praises the same hero as B.40; which may itself be a secondary alteration. It is obscure and corrupt. It begins by saying 'His hand used to feed [carrion-]birds; I honour him. . . . He put on gold [ornaments], in the van of combat, in the fierce struggle. . . .'

It then calls him '. . . one of the Three Fearful Ones, the pursuer of the battle-shout, the terrible bear . . . the terrifier of champions . . .', and ends '. . . Handsome was Cibno son of Gwengad.' The 'Three Fearful Ones' is a reference to a 'triad', on which see the Introduction § 15 at the end. This triad actually exists (see TYP., p. 196), but it does not include Cibno. Perhaps the present passage means merely that he was worthy to be one of them; at any rate it bears witness to the existence of the triad in the ninth to tenth centuries, if not the sixth.

B.42 = CA. lxvii B

See the note on B.39. This verse consists of two lines only, breaking off in the middle of the last word of the second line at the bottom of p. 38 of the MS.; see the Introduction § 13. For the original continuation see the variant A.66.

'A most fitting song of a skilful company. A pleasant little place in the world, he was not covetous [of it (?)].'

The Later Text A

'This is the *Gododdin*; Aneirin sang it.'

A.1 = CA. i

This famous verse begins the MS. and has always hitherto been treated as the opening of the whole poem. 'Worked (?) gold'; the meaning of *aphan* is uncertain, but the treatment in BBCS. XI, 33, seems quite unconvincing. 'A beloved friend', see BBCS. XVII, 93 f. The words 'that he is under a cairn' (lit. 'stones') is my emendation; the MS. reads *vrein* 'ravens', for which I suggest *vein* 'stones', on the grounds (1) that *vrein* has already occurred as rhyme-word three lines before, which is a metrical impropriety; (2) that the scribe intended to write *vein* but his eye was caught by *vrein* above; (3) that '*under* ravens' for 'perched on [and eaten] by ravens' is a little forced; (4) that *a dan vein* 'under stones', i.e. buried beneath a cairn, occurs elsewhere in very early Welsh poetry (CLH., p. 14, v. 22), along with parallel phrases meaning 'buried' such as 'under clay and sand' (v. 25). Note that the first nineteen verses of the A. text have no variants.

'A man in vigour, a boy in years, boisterous in courage; there were swift thick-maned horses under the thigh of the handsome youth, with a light broad shield on the crupper of his slender speedy [horse]; bright blue swords [and] fringes of worked (?) gold. There shall be no hatred between you and me, I shall do better with you – praise you in song. He would sooner have gone to the battlefield than to a wedding, he would sooner have been food for ravens than get due burial. A beloved friend was Ywain, it is a shame that he is under a cairn. I marvel in what land the slaying of the only son of Marro could come to pass.'

A.2 = CA. ii

This begins a chain of four verses starting 'Wearing a brooch' (on 'brooch' here see the Introduction § 10), three of which add 'in the front rank'. 'Breathless in the presence of a girl' means that in spite of his fierceness in battle Madog was modest with women. For '*where* he pursued' see BBCS. XIII, 205; for '*who* did not flee', *Llen Cymru* VI, 239; VII, 113; VIII, 136; BBCS. XIII, 188. The last sentence seems to mean that whenever Madog took part in a battle he killed ninety-nine out of a hundred of the enemy; or perhaps that he and his men fought furiously till one alone remained alive. It is evident it cannot be a reference to the Gododdin survivors of Catraeth. 'The men of Gododdin recount' could well be translated 'The *Gododdin* recounts', as elsewhere in this poem, but as the reference is not to Catraeth the former is perhaps better here. 'On the floor of the palace' would refer to the company feasting at tables in the hall, in that case, rather than to the reciter standing up before the company. The same passage occurs at the end of A.68, where it seems out of place.

> 'Wearing a brooch, in the front rank wherever he went, breathless in the presence of a girl, he earned his mead. The front of his shield was pierced; when he heard the battle-cry he gave no quarter where he pursued; he would not come back from fight till the blood had flowed, like rushes he cut down the men who did not flee. The men of Gododdin recount on the floor of the palace that when he used to come back to Madog's tent there used not to return but one in a hundred.'

A.3 = CA. iii

'The net of the enemy' means he trapped them. It is very doubtful whether 'the land of Manawyd' can be Manaw (the word translated 'land' may mean 'battle'), but the reference seems in any case to be to some battle won by

Cadfannan. 'Unless . . . nourished' should mean that none but a strong well-fed warrior could parry Cadfannan's blows.

'Wearing a brooch, a warrior, the net of the enemy, with the swoop of an eagle in the river-mouths when it has been fed, his pledge was a promise that was kept – he did better, his purpose was not turned back. Before the army of Gododdin there was a panic retreat, a bold drive before the land (?) of Manawyd. Neither beauty (?) nor a shield was a protection, and unless one had been well-nourished it was not possible to withstand Cadfannan's blow.'

A.4 = CA. iv

On the name Gwefrfawr see Ellis Evans, *Gaulish Personal Names* (Cardiff, 1967), p. 272 n. For '[giving]' read perhaps '[deserving, receiving]'.

'Wearing a brooch, in the front rank, like a wolf in fury, [giving] amber beads [and] spurs (?) [and] torques at the share-out, Gwefrfawr was invaluable in return for wine from the drinking-horn; he drove back the assault with blood down his cheeks. Though the men of Gwynedd and the North should come against his land, through the stratagem of the son of Ysgyrran their shields would be broken.'

A.5 = CA. v

'Wearing a brooch, in the front rank, armed in the battle shout, a mighty man in combat before his [death-]day, a leader charging forwards before armies; there fell five times fifty before his blades, of the men of Deira and Bernicia there fell a hundred score, they were annihilated in one hour. He would sooner be flesh for wolves than go to a wedding, he would sooner be prey for the raven than go to the altar, he would sooner his blood flowed to the ground than that he should get due burial,

in return for mead in the hall among the hosts. Hyfaidd
the tall shall be honoured as long as there is a minstrel.'

A.6 = CA. vi

Here begins a chain of nine verses beginning 'the men went'
(verses 13–14, 'the man went', and also in 12, emending
gwyr to *gwr*, which seems needed there). All but 6 and 7,
which have 'to Gododdin', continue 'to Catraeth', and
10–14 add 'with the dawn' or 'with the day'. 'To Gododdin' looks like a mistake for 'to Catraeth', but it is supported by metre and internal rhyme. A.21 and 33 are
evidently misplaced and must have belonged originally to
this chain. 'Inciting to laughter', that is, in hilarious mood.
The last clause may also be translated 'true is the tale,
death overtook them', but this is so feeble that it does not
deserve to be right, and a recent argument in favour of it
in BBCS. XIII, 189 is not conclusive since it can be used
equally well to support the other translation.

> 'The men went to Gododdin, inciting [one another] to
> laughter, bitter with spears in battle, drawing them-
> selves up in ranks; for a short year at peace they were
> undisturbed. The son of Bodgad, the deeds of his hand
> wrought vengeance. Though they should go to churches
> to do penance, both old and young, both strong and
> puny, the inescapable tryst with death overtook them.'

A.7 = CA. vii

> 'The men went to Gododdin, fierce in their laughter,
> attacking in the army, eager for fight; they slew with
> their blades without much noise. Rheithfyw the pillar
> of battle delighted in giving [gifts].'

A.8 = CA. viii

> 'The men went to Catraeth, swift was their host, the
> pale mead was their feast and it was their poison; three

hundred fighting according to plan, and after the jubilation [of battle] there was silence. Though they should
go to churches to do penance, the inescapable tryst with
death overtook them.'

A.9 = CA. ix

'The young son of Cian' is clearly the Llif or Llifiau of B.13
and A.22. Maen Gwyngwn is unknown, but since he was
from 'beyond Bannog' it would be in Pictland somewhere.
'In close ranks', lit. 'compactly, densely'. 'Wanted no dowry'
means he was interested only in fighting, not in getting
married; cf. A.5.

'The men went to Catraeth, fed on mead, . . . , sturdy
and vigorous – it would be unfitting if I did not tell of
them – along with great red blades with dark-blue
sockets; in close ranks and stubbornly the bloodhounds
fought. I should have judged it overburdening for the
bodyguard of Bernicia; I should not have left alive
anyone in man's shape. I have lost a friend [to whom]
I was loyal, one swift in the struggle, rugged, ever foremost. The brave man wanted no father-in-law's dowry,
the young son of Cian from Maen Gwyngwn.'

A.10 = CA. x

The name of the hero referred to in the last sentence is
missing; a line has probably dropped out. The second
clause means that if they had any fears, they vanished once
they set off.

'The men went to Catraeth with the dawn, their fears
shifted their abode (?); a hundred thousand and three
hundred cast at each other, bloodily they splashed spears.
His was the bravest station in combat, in front of the
retinue of Mynyddog the Luxurious.'

A.11 = CA. xi

'Their mettle shortened their lives', i.e. their courageous

spirit brought about their early death. 'Never be cleansed', perhaps 'May the men of Gododdin always have plenty of fighting'? On the 'square-pointed spear-heads' see BBCS. VI, 314.

> 'The men went to Catraeth with the dawn, their mettle shortened their lives. They drank sweet, yellow ensnaring mead; for a year many a minstrel was glad. Red were their swords, may their spears never be cleansed; [there were] lime-white shields and square-pointed spear-heads before the retinue of Mynyddog the Luxurious.'

A.12 = CA. xii

'They made biers a certainty', i.e. they ensured the death of the enemy. On Neirthiad see the Introduction, § 5. The last four words mean he planned some brave tactical move.

> 'The man went to Catraeth with the day, he brought disgrace on battalions. With great blades, giving no quarter in the world, they made biers a certainty. He made a bath of blood and the death of his opponent sooner than speak of truce. When he moved in front of the army of Gododdin Neirthiad the brave made a bold design.'

A.13 = CA. xiii

On Tudfwlch see the Introduction § 8. 'Every seventh day' must refer not to Catraeth but to previous attacks on the English. 'Slaughter-ring', lit. 'blood-enclosure'; the enemy were surrounded and massacred.

> 'The man went to Catraeth with the day; he drank up the mead-carousal at midnight. Hapless was his expedition, the lament of his fellow warriors, the fiery killer. No great man whose boasts were so expansive . . . sped forth to Catraeth; there was none who put the enemy to flight from the stronghold of Eidyn so utterly as he, Tudfwlch the tall, from its land and its steadings; he slew the Saxons every seventh day. Long (?) shall [remembrance of] his valour last, and memories of him

among his fair company. When Tudfwlch arrived, the strengthener of his people, the son of Cilydd, there was a slaughter-ring in the place of spears.'

A.14 = CA. xiv

'In his battle-square he was a fence of shields', see the Introduction § 9. This depends on an emendation, and taking the resulting *budyn*, 'cattle pen', relatively literally; contrast BIK., p. 198, where Jarman accepts the emendation but interprets it differently. The same word occurs in the same sense in A.17. 'Competitive', lit. 'jealous'; 'weapons', lit. 'irons'.

'The man went to Catraeth with the dawn, in his battle-square (?) he was a fence of shields; they attacked harshly, they collected booty, the noise of their shields was loud, like thunder. A competitive man, a sagacious man, a lone champion; he slashed and pierced with spears, above the . . . in [battle-]straits he struck with blades, steel weapons on the heads [of men, but] in the palace the slayer was mild. Before Erthgi armies groaned.'

A.15 = CA. xv

The 'sons of Godebog' mentioned in this verse are generally supposed to represent the Northern dynasties claiming descent from Coel Hen Godebog, whose floruit would have been early in the fifth century according to the genealogies. The kings of Rheged, including Urien, were one of these lines. The passage seems to hint at hostility between Gododdin and some region of SW. Scotland, but nothing is known of this.

'The recital concerns the land (?) of Catraeth. The host fell, long was the grief for them. Whether with hardship or with ease, they used to defend their land against the sons of Godebog, a wicked folk. Long biers carried off bloodstained men; it was a pitiful fate, a true compulsion, that was doomed for Tudfwlch and Cyfwlch the tall. Though we drank bright mead by the light of tapers, though its taste was good its bitterness was long-lasting.'

A.16 = CA. xvi

'Blaen from the spacious (?), splendid city used to urge on the faithful warriors who followed him. [Reclining] on his cushions, Blaen used to dispense the drinking-horn in his luxurious palace; there was drink of bragget for Blaen; Blaen delighted in gold and purple [robes]; well-fed horses used to gallop with Blaen upon them, obeying his harsh voice – his mettle deserved all these. Blaen used to raise the shout of battle, returning with booty; he was a bear in the pathway, it was long ere *he* would retreat.'

A.17 = CA. xvii

On '[the fight at] the ford' see the Introduction § 9; scarcely 'the water of the ford was made rough' by the hero charging into it, and certainly still less the pointless proverb envisaged in CA., p. 120. 'Like a cattle-pen', cf. A.14. 'Like a leek'; the simile is obscure, but the same occurs also often in the Edda. '*In* broil', cf. BBCS. XVII, 149 f. There are a number of obscurities in this verse.

'With violence in his post in the front rank, like a fierce sun; where is the prince to be found, the lord of the island of Britain? Rough was the [fight at the] ford in the face of the harsh one with his shield like a cattle-pen (?). His drinking-horn was handsome in the hall of Eidyn; his kingliness was spectacular, his mead was intoxicating, he drank wine-drink, he was a reaper in combat, he drank sweet (?) wine. Bold of purpose in battle, a reaper like a leek in battle; bright arm of battle, they sang (?) a song (?) of battle; armoured in battle, winged in battle, his shield was not [left] broad by the spears of war. His contemporaries fell in the war-fight;

unhurt in the broil, he avenged them irreproachably. His frenzy was appeased, before the grave of Gwrfelling the great had a green surface.'

A.18 = CA. xviii

The word rendered here 'lawful entitlements' is difficult to translate; it is a legal term for the honourable characteristics the possession of which entitled a person or thing to its full status in law or qualified it to hold that status; not quite 'rights' or 'privileges'. The line seems to imply that the three heroes were upholders of the established socio-legal system. 'On the path of', see BBCS. XI, 148 f.

'They respected lawful entitlements, they stained three spear-shafts – [rather,] fifty and five hundred. Three hounds with three hundred, three . . . battle-horsemen of Eidyn of the many goldsmiths; three hosts wearing mail-coats; three lords wearing gold torques, three bold horsemen, three battle-peers, three equal chiefs (?) bounding forwards together; they routed the enemy bitterly. Three in fight, in hardship, they slew . . . easily (?); like gold in the close-packed battle, three lords of the people who sprang of the Britons – Cynri and Cynon and Cynrain of Aeron. The heathen, the crafty men of Deira, used to ask whether there [ever] came of the Britons a man better than Cynon, the serpent on the path of the enemy.'

A.19 = CA. xix

A.19 and 20 make a chain beginning 'I drank wine and mead in the palace'; however the context in A.20 (q.v.) shows the 2nd sg. is needed there, and it should therefore very likely be read here too. 'Athrwys' and 'Affrai' appear to be intended as names, and the first is in fact a known Welsh name, though not the second. They are not likely to be members of the Northumbrian army, none of whose names are known elsewhere; possibly this is a reference to some famous feat in a previous civil combat among the Britons.

'I drank wine and mead in the palace. Great was the number of his spears (?) in the encounter of men; he made food for eagles. When Cydywal hastened out he raised the battle-cry with the green dawn; wherever (?) he went he left shields splintered and broken; slashing at them, he cut off tough spears in battle, he crushed the van of the army; the son of Sywno (the soothsayer foreknew it) sold his life that his glory might be told forth. He struck with sharpened blade, he slew both Athrwys (?) and Affrai (?); because of his pledge he premeditated attack, he caused there to be corpses of brave men of war, he charged forwards in the forefront of the men of Gwynedd.'

A.20 = CA. xx A

This is a variant of B.12, q.v. The first three verbs are in the first singular, but the second singular is obviously needed, which makes it probable that we should substitute this in the first line of A.19. 'Because you did not flee'; the MS. has *phechut* 'sin' in place of *thechut* 'flee', but the reading of B (*thechut*), substituted here, is obviously right because much more in keeping with the ethics of the Heroic Age; the Christian context however made some scribe of later times substitute 'sin'. The name of the hero is Breichiol in B.12, which is probably the better reading.

'You drank wine and mead in the palace; since you drank, you attacked in the border region, a lamentable fate. Not un-destructive was [your] fierce heart (?). When everyone else fled you attacked; may you have the joyful land [of Heaven] because you did not flee; Breichior the fierce was world-famed.'

A.21 = CA. xxi

This verse belongs to the chain A.6–14 (and A.33), see the

note on A.6. 'The two battle-hounds of Aeron' are perhaps Cynri and Cynrain, see A.18.

> 'The men went to Catraeth, they were famous; wine and mead from golden vessels was their drink for a year, according to the honourable custom; three men and three score and three hundred wearing gold torques. Of those that hastened forth after the choice drink none escaped but three, through feats of combat; the two battle-hounds of Aeron and Cynon the stubborn (?) – and I, with my blood streaming down, for the sake of my brilliant poetry.'

A.22 = CA. xxii A

See B.13 on the relation between the two verses. 'The harsh dragon' is Mynyddog; on 'dragon' see the Introduction, § 12, at the end. 'After the swordstroke' must mean *in* battle, not after the battle was over (cf. B.13), since to be harsh in that case would be inconsistent with the heroic ethos. 'The men of Gododdin'; or, 'the *Gododdin*'.

> 'My kinsman, my very gentle one (?), does not cause us anxiety, unless it were because of the feast of the harsh dragon; he was not excluded from the mead-drink in the hall. He used to make destruction upon destruction with many blows, he was dauntless in battle and dauntless in affliction. The men of Gododdin do not tell of anyone more harsh than Llifiau after the swordstroke.'

A.23 = CA. xxiii A

On the relation between this verse and B.11 see the note on B.11. Both verses consist of five long-lines. The first two long-lines in A.23 are in a rhyme different from that of the rest of the verse, the rest being the same as the rhyme all through B.11; and further, the first two-thirds of the first long-line of A.23 are the same as the beginning of the Gorchan of Tudfwlch. The last two long-lines are a variant

of the last two of B.11 (with a different hero, however);
but there is nothing in common between not only the first
two long-lines but even the third of A.23 and B.11, in spite
of the fact that the rhyme is the same in the two third
long-lines. It would appear that A.23 has wrongly acquired
the beginning of the Gorchan of Tudfwlch and the end of
B.11, the first helped by the fact that the metre is the same
and the second by the fact that the rhyme is the same.

> 'When the weapons were scattered and the ranks broken,
> unshaken and with great destruction the lone champion
> routed the English rabble; he showered shafts in the
> front rank of the fray, in the javelin-fight. He made men
> prostrate and women widows before his death. Graid
> son of Hoewgi used to form the battle-pen in the pres-
> ence of the spears.'

A.24 = CA. xxiv

'The eagle of the graceful swoop' is Buddfan, and 'his
proposals deprived him of the rights' means that his bold
schemes for battle brought about the loss of his rights and
of his existence as a man; i.e., his death. It is uncertain
whether Eleirch is a place.

> 'The warrior of the protective (?) shield . . . and with
> the gallop of a colt, he was an uproar on the battle slope,
> he was a fire, his spears were impetuous, were flashing;
> he was the food of ravens, he was prey for ravens; and
> before the eagle of the graceful swoop was left at the
> fords with the falling of the dew, and by the spray of
> the wave beside the hill, the bards of the world judged
> him to be of manly heart. His proposals deprived him
> of his rights, his chief warriors were destroyed by the
> men [of the enemy]; and before he was buried under
> the hill of Eleirch (?) – there was courage in his breast –
> his blood washed over his armour, Buddfan the intrepid
> son of Bleiddfan.'

A.25 = CA. xxv

'Ample feats'; it is very improbable that *camb* (probably =
camp, 'feat') could be the archaic form of *cam* 'crooked', as
this would require a written text going back virtually to
the time of Aneirin himself. 'He did not leave', etc., means
he was never willingly absent from the great New Year
feast at his court, when gifts were traditionally given by
the chief to minstrels (among others). 'His land was not
ploughed though it were uninhabited' is unclear; does it
mean he is praised for keeping uninhabited land waste
and hunting in it, a hero's peacetime occupation and more
noble than concerning himself with agriculture like a boor?
On 'wyvern' and 'dragon' see Introduction § 12, end.

> 'It would be wrong to leave him without memorial, him
> of the ample feats (?) who used not to desert the breach
> through cowardice. He did not leave his court of set
> purpose on the Calends of January, a profit to the
> minstrels of Britain. His land was not ploughed though
> it were uninhabited, the very hostile one in tumult, the
> generous wyvern, the dragon in bloodshed after the
> wine-feast – Gwenabwy son of Gwen – in the conflict
> at Catraeth.'

A.26 = CA. xxvi A

See the variant B.18 and the notes on it; it is only half the
length of A.26, but it is impossible to say which is the more
original in this, as also whether 'Cadlew' or 'Tudlew' is
right. The point of being 'reared by the gates' is obscure.
The 'reaping party' is reaping in haste before the storm.

> 'It was true as Cadlew said (?), no one's horses could
> overtake Marchlew. He showered spears in fight from
> his bounding, wide-coursing [horse]. Though he were
> not reared by the gates, by the gate (?), his swordstroke
> was bold in his [battle-]station (?). He showered ash
> spears from the five fingers of his hand, from his slender
> steaming chestnut [horse]. The very dear one distributed

his wine in plenty; he slew with a stained fierce blade, as when a reaping-party strikes in unsettled weather; Marchlew used to make streams of blood.'

A.27 = CA. xxvii

'Isag' is the Biblical name Isaac, part of the evidence for the Christianity of the men of Gododdin. 'From the region of the South' does not necessarily mean he was a Welshman, of course; he could have been from Rheged or Elfed. To a Welshman, *o barth deheu* naturally suggests *Deheubarth*, South Wales, but this would not be natural to a Gododdin man. Compare the usage in Scotland at the present day, whereby 'the South' is often employed to mean 'England'. 'Requital was abandoned', that is, when once he had stabbed an enemy no further fighting was needed; 'he was not by turns', etc., see Caerwyn Williams in BBCS. XVI, 105 ff.

> 'Isag the distinguished man from the region of the South, his manners were like the sea-flood for graciousness and liberality and pleasant mead-drinking. Where his weapons gouged requital was abandoned; he was not by turns cruel and un-cruel nor guileful (?) and guileless (?); his sword echoed in the heads of mothers; the rampart of fury, he was renowned, the son of Gwydd-nau.'

A.28 = CA. xxviii

'The fosterling', see David Greene in *Celtica*, II, 338.

> 'Ceredig whose fame was precious, he seized and kept renown, the fosterling, he was serene before his [death-]day came; his refined manners were perfection. May the friend of the arts have an assignation in the land of Heaven, the home of enlightenment.'

A.29 = CA. xxix

'Ceredig the beloved chieftain, a furious champion in

battle, the gold-filigreed shield of the battle-field, with broken spears in splinters and a bold mighty sword-stroke. Like a man he used to stand his ground among spears; before the grief of burial, before the suffering, he used to defend his post by design. May he have a welcome among the host [of Heaven] in perfect union with the Trinity.'

A.30 = CA. xxx

'Fed the wolves', that is, by providing them with corpses; cf. the Introduction § 12, end. Bryn Hyddwn, an unknown hill, but the context suggests it was in the neighbourhood of Catraeth.

'When Caradog hastened forth to battle like a wild boar, cutting down three heroes, the bull of the army, striking down in combat, he fed the wolves by his hand. My witness was Ywain son of Eulad and Gwrien and Gwyn and Gwriad, before they were taken from Catraeth, from the slaughter, from Bryn Hyddwn; after bright mead in the hand, not one of them saw his father [again].'

A.31 = CA. xxxi

This verse makes a chain with A.32 on the theme 'The men hastened forth, they were . . . together.' Gwgon and Gwion reappear in A.81.

'The men hastened forth, they were bounding forwards together, short-lived they were, drunk over the clari-fied mead, the retinue of Mynyddog famous in [battle-] straits; their lives were payment for their feast of mead. Caradog and Madog, Pyll and Ieuan, Gwgon and Gwion, Gwyn and Cynfan, Peredur of the steel weapons, Gwawrddur and Aeddan, who rushed forwards in battle among broken shields; and though they were slain they slew, none returned to his lands.'

A.32 = CA. xxxii

On Gwlyged see the Introduction, § 5.

'The men hastened forth, they were feasted together for a year over the mead; great were their boasts. How sad to tell of them, what insatiable longing! Cruel was their resting-place; no mother's son succoured them. How long was the grief for them and the yearning, after the fiery men from the lands of wine-feasting! For the spirited men, Gwlyged of Gododdin contrived the famous feast of Mynyddog – and the costly, when paid for by the battle (?) at Catraeth.'

A.33 = CA. xxxiii

As already noted, this verse really belongs with A.6–14 (and A.21).

'The men went to Catraeth in a battalion, with the war-cry; a force of horses with dark blue armour and shields, shafts held aloft and sharp spears and bright mail-coats and swords. He took the lead, he burst through armies, five times fifty fell before his blades; Rhufon the tall, he presented gold to the altar and gifts and fine presents to the minstrel.'

A.34 = CA. xxxiv

A.34, 35, and 36 make a chain on the theme 'Never was built a hall so . . . ,' and A.57 is a misplaced member of it. The hall is Mynyddog's. The verse appears to celebrate three heroes. It may be noted that Gwid, in its Pictish form Wid, was the name of the father of three kings of the Picts who died in the years 635, 641, and 653 respectively, so that chronologically he could well be the same person.

'Never was built a hall so full of clamour, so great – and whose disaster was so very great. You deserved to enjoy your mead, fiery (?) Morien. He did not tell that Cynon would not make a corpse, the armoured spearman of far-reaching fame. His sword rang on the stockade; Gwid son of Peithan no more trembled than trembles a rock of vast circumference (?).'

A.35 = CA. xxxv

'Who set fire' etc. is either figurative or means that the anonymous son of Fferog caused the enemy to strike sparks from their horseshoes in flight.

'Never was built a hall so famous. Except for Morien, a worthy successor to Caradog, no bold man escaped like a lord in [battle-]stress who was bolder than the son of Fferog, whose hand was mighty, who set fire under the fleeing horseman, brave in the tumult, a very fortress for a panic-stricken host; before the army of Gododdin his shield was shattered, he was steadfast in affliction. On the day of wrath he was agile, truly his recompense was bitter; he deserved his horns of mead, the liegeman of Mynyddog.'

A.36 = CA. xxxvi

A.57 shows that this is Cynon son of Clydno of Eidyn. There appears to be a line missing after the first one, since the next sentence begins '*than* Cynon'. 'At the end of the couch', see the Introduction § 10.

'Never was built a hall so durable. Cynon of the generous heart, the bejewelled (?) prince, he sat at the end of the couch; whoever he struck needed no second blow. Very sharp were his spears; with lime-white shield hacked small, he burst through armies; very swift were his horses, he charged before all; on the day of wrath his blades were destructive, when Cynon sped forth with the green dawn.'

A.37 = CA. xxxviii

This verse forms a chain with A.38 and 39, the first two being closer to each other than to 39. B.30 also belongs to

this chain, and its first line is close to that of A.39, though
B.30 praises Eithinyn like A.37 and 38 but unlike 39. On
A.53 see A.38. 'Elffin' is unknown, though the name, from
Latin Alpinus, is found elsewhere in early Scottish history;
thus Ywain the victor at Strathcarron in 642 had a son
and a third cousin of this name, and there is also the Alpín
father of 'Kenneth mac Alpine'.

> 'He attacked in [battle-]stress in the forefront, he drove
> out the oppressor, he fixed the boundary; the lord who
> struck with spears, laughing in war, . . . , his courage
> like Elffin; Eithinyn the renowned, the rampart of fury,
> the bull of battle.'

A.38 = CA. xxxix A

See the note on A.37. A.53 is really a close variant of A.38,
but it has got absorbed into a different chain, and provided
with the first line of that chain, owing to faulty memory
and the fact that the rhyme is the same. It really belongs
here.

> 'He attacked in [battle-]stress in the forefront in return
> for mead in the hall and drink of wine. He showered his
> blades between the two armies, the distinguished horse-
> man, in front of the men of Gododdin; Eithinyn the re-
> nowned, the rampart of fury, the bull of battle.'

A.39 = CA. xlii

See the note on A.37. There are a number of obscurities in
this verse. 'Beli' is unknown; it looks as if a cattle-raid had
been made on Cadfannan's lands and he had repulsed it.
On Cadfannan see A.3 and 61. 'Lawful entitlements', see
the note on A.18.

> 'He attacked in [battle-]stress for the cattle-herds of the
> East, a host with . . . shields arose (?); [there was] a
> broken shield before the cattle of Beli the boisterous.
> The lord in the bloodshed, hastening on the border, the
> grey-haired one who sustained us, on his front-line

skittish steed, in rugged shape, the ox, wearing a gold torque; the boar, the wily one made a compact in front of the boundary, worthy of his lawful entitlements, confronting the war-cry; let Him who calls us to Heaven be. . . . He shakes his battle-spears in fight, Cadfannan famous . . . booty, it was not disputed (?) that an army would be humbled (?) before him.'

A.40 = CA. xliii A

See the variant B.5. A.40 makes a chain with A.41, or is perhaps an extremely loose variant of it; cf. B.5–6. See the note on B.5. Like that of the other three, the beginning is unclear. 'The eagle', see Introduction, § 12, at the end. On Myrddin see the Introduction § 14; 'the blessed inspiration of Myrddin' means Welsh poetry, = Celtic civilisation?

'For the very wretched . . . , for the smiling land and the waste, for the falling of the hair from the head from the men of the eagle, Gwyddien the fierce (?), he defended it with his spear, the marshaller, the tamer, its owner. Morien defended the blessed inspiration of Myrddin, and laid the head of the chief in the earth with our help. . . . Bradwen [fought like] three men to please his love; [like] twelve, Gwenabwy son of Gwen.'

A.41 = CA. xliv A

See the variant B.6, and the note on A.40. Morien has dropped out of this verse, and also Gwenabwy; see the note on B.5.

'For the very wretched . . . , struggling vigorously with the shields in fight and swordstrokes on the head; men cut down in England before the three hundred chiefs. He who may hold on to the mane of a wolf without a spear in his hand must always have a bold spirit under his mantle. In the wrathful and destructive conflict Bradwen died, he did not escape.'

A.42 = CA. xlv A

This short verse is a variant of B.25 and 35. Like them, it is corrupt and difficult. It ends, 'Still others tell of the adventures of the chief, about his brilliant mould. No others tell that Cynhafal was not an ally at the hour of cockcrow.'

A.43 = CA. xlvi

'When you were a famous warrior, defending the corn of the borderlands (?), for our merits we were called illustrious men of mark. He was an unyielding gate, an unyielding fortress of refuge; he was civil to the suppliant who approached him, he was a fortress for the army who trusted him; none called on Gwynfyd but he would be there.'

A.44 = CA. xlvii

The verse is an interpolated *englyn* taken from the cycle of Llywarch Hen and his sons; see the Introduction § 14. On 'the end of the bench' see § 10; the word for 'bench' is borrowed from Anglo-Saxon, which supports the view that the verse is late.

'Though there were a hundred men in the one house, I recognise the sorrows of Cyny; the chief of men, he was worthy of the end of the bench.'

A.45 = CA. xlviii

On this verse and the next see the Introduction § 14. In CA., pp. 205 ff. Williams takes the words in brackets to mean that in his inspired ecstasy the poet stands outside himself and does not know himself, and that his contemporary the bard Taliesin well understands the nature of this experience. This seems rather unconvincing; and compare § 14 above. The first words of the verse mean that the poet, lying underground, is not a tired nobleman reclining comfortably on a couch.

'I am no weary lord; I am unable to take vengeance for provocation, I do not laugh a laugh, under the feet of maggots; my knee is stretched out in an underground dwelling, there is an iron chain around my knees. About the mead, about the drinking-horn, about the folk at Catraeth, I Aneirin (and yet not I; Taliesin of the skilful declamation knows it) sang the *Gododdin* before the dawn of the following (?) day.'

A.46 = CA. xlix

On Cenau son of Llywarch Hen see the Introduction § 5.

'The valour of the North, he was one who displayed it, with generous heart, the lord who was bountiful by his nature. There does not travel the earth, mother has not borne, one so handsome and strong in his iron armour. By the might of his bright sword he rescued me, from the barbarous underground prison he took me, from the place of death, from the cruel land – Cenau son of Llywarch, bold and daring.'

A.47 = CA. l

Senyllt (father of Nudd 'the Generous'), who belonged to the royal families of southern Scotland, was traditionally one of the Triad of 'The Three Generous Ones' of Britain; see TYP., p. 5 f. Here, Heilyn's court is compared to Senyllt's for liberality; the context shows that the particular 'reproach' envisaged would have been for stinting supplies of mead. For 'Gododdin' here, Williams would substitute 'Deira', because the line is too long as it stands.

'The court of Senyllt did not suffer reproach, with its vessels full of mead. He used to mete out the sword to wrong-doers (?), he used to mete out swooping [assaults] (?) in war; he carried away bloodstained men in his arms in the presence of the army of Gododdin and the men of Bernicia. In his hall there were wont to be swift horses, bloody spears, and dark-blue armour; a long yellow spear (?) in his hand, and in his wrath there was haste. Smiling and smiling at random, and ceasing at times, unkind and kind by turns, whose men were not apt to show their heels in flight; Heilyn who assaulted every borderland.'

A.48 = CA. li A

See the variants B.3 and 24, and particularly the note on B.3. This version is only less obscure. It begins 'A slab of rock in cleared country, in cleared country a hill, [on the] borderland of Gododdin . . . ,' and speaks of 'the warrior-band from Din Dywyd which came to us, which came upon us;' and continues, 'they pleaded earnestly, they struck bitterly, thoroughly they caused suffering to the [enemy] host; the shield of Grugyn, it was broken-fronted before the bull of battle.'

A.49 = CA. lii

The verse is full of difficulties. For a somewhat different rendering of the last sentence see Rowlands in *Llen Cymry* VI, 240. It begins 'His enemies fear his weapon, the combative eagle, laughing aloud in battle', and after a number of obscure clauses, continues, 'With lively speed, Rhys spent freely on ostentation (?); not so, those who will not achieve their purpose. Those whom he chanced to overtake will not escape.'

A.50 = CA. liii

It is very unclear what this verse is about. Williams takes *dy wr* 'thy man' as a mistake for *Dewr*, 'a man of Deira', and emends *llaw* 'hand' to *llogell* 'bag, purse', and understands the end as 'may he rarely have profit in his purse'; he envisages Cynwal as driving the Deirans into hiding where they live on what poor food they can snatch. This all seems rather forced; is it not rather that Cynwal took part in an unlucky expedition on horseback and was forced to go on the run, which the poet hopes will not last long?

But if so this would suggest an interpolation in the poem
from some story about Cynwal's previous life.

'It was with ill luck that the shield which kindly Cynwal
bore (?) was pierced, it was with ill luck that he laid his
thigh across the long-legged slender grey. Yellow was
his spear, yellow; yellower was his saddle. Your man is
in his hut gnawing the leg of a buck, the spoils of his
hand; may it be a rare thing for him.'

A.51 = CA. liv A

This is a variant of B.7; see the note on that verse. The end
of B.7 is obscure, but A.51 is somewhat clearer, and seems
to mean that Addonwy did not live long enough to see
himself avenged.

'Good was the fortune, Addonwy, I know, which you
had promised me, that what Bradwen did you would
do; you would slay, you would burn, you would do no
worse than Morien. You did not hold out long, on the
wing or the van. [Though your] eye [was] bold and not
blindfolded, you did not see the great fury of the horsemen; they slew, they gave no quarter to the Saxons.'

A.52 = CA. lv A

This is a variant of B.2, the 'reciter's preface', q.v. Drum
Esyd is an unidentified place, though one would suppose
it close to Edinburgh. 'Desirous of silver' means the reciter
hopes to win the prize; the *teaching* of the son of Dwywai
is his poetry. The reciter describes the hospitable hall of
Eidyn where Aneirin lived, but B.2 suggests this is a later
accretion. 'From dusk to dusk' may also be 'from dawn to
dusk' or 'from dusk to dawn', but the speaker is more
likely to praise the great hall (where the retainers slept as
well as passed the daytime) for its hospitality all through
the twenty-four hours.

'*Gododdin*, I claim your support, [in] the valleys beyond

the ridges of Drum Esyd, [I] a youth desirous of silver without reproach (?), by the teaching of the son of Dwywai of high courage. He was not weak of counsel, or base, before the well-fed fire, the pine-logs blazing from dusk to dusk, the lit-up doorway [open] for the purple-clad traveller. The slaying of the gentle one, the killing of the courteous one, the rampart of battle – Aneirin and his poetry were not to be parted.'

A.53 = CA. xxxix B

A.54–56 make a chain beginning 'The uprising of (skilful) warriors', and A.53, which is really a variant of A.38 and belongs in the chain A.37–39, has been given the same opening line as A.54 and 55 (presumably because its rhyme all through it is the same as that of that line) and then misplaced into that chain. A.53 is identical throughout with A.38, except that for the one line 'He attacked in [battle-] stress in the forefront' of A.38, A.53 gives two lines 'The uprising of skilful warriors to Catraeth, a swift spirited army'; and then continues 'in return for mead' etc., exactly as in A.38.

A.54 = CA. lvi

The verse has a number of obscurities. It begins: 'The uprising of skilful warriors of a mighty (?) land', and after some difficult lines it continues 'The worthy lord does not come to terms with provocation, Morial does not endure reproach in the pursuit, he with the steel blades ready for bloodshed.'

A.55 = CA. lvii

The whole verse is only four lines, of which the first is 'The uprising of skilful warriors of a mighty (?) land', but the rest is too doubtful to hazard a complete translation. No hero is named.

A.56 = CA. lviii

'The uprising of warriors, they gathered together, together with single purpose they attacked; short were
their lives, long the grief for them among their kinsmen;
they slew seven times as many of the English. In battle
they made women widows, [and] many a mother with
tears at her eyelids.'

A.57 = CA. xxxvii

This is a misplaced member of the chain A.34–36, being
closest to A.36; see the note on A.34. As in A.36, there
appears to be a line missing after the first one, since the
'*as* Cynon' at the beginning of the third, constructed with
'As bountiful' etc. of the second, makes no sense without a
comparison; perhaps something like 'nor was there ever a
bold man' (*glew*). Since *mor* can also be exclamative 'how!'
this too would solve it if *a* at the beginning of the third is
assumed to be a mistake for some other monosyllable; and
it is so taken here. 'Like a fortress;' he rallied the waverers
there.

'Never was built a hall so faultless. . . . How bountiful,
in fury like a lion, most widely-travelled, was Cynon
of the generous heart, the noble and most fair! His war-
cry on the furthest wings was like a fortress, the gate, the
anchor of the army, the plundering chieftain. Of all I
have seen and shall see in fight, plying their weapons
in the battle-shout, his valour was the boldest; he slew
the enemy with the sharpest blade, like rushes they fell
before his hand. Son of Clydno of enduring fame, to
you, lord, I sing; fame without bounds, without limit.'

A.58 = CA. lix

This makes a chain with A.59 and 60 on the theme 'After
wine-feast and mead-feast'; see B.20. There are numerous
obscurities in this verse, and it can only be summarised. It

begins 'After wine-feast and mead-feast they dispensed (?) slaughter (?)'; there is reference to the (apparently anonymous) hero 'before the front of Buddugre' (apparently a place name, 'Victorious Hill'), and to 'ravens soaring and mounting to the clouds' and 'warriors falling on him like a grey swarm without making him retreat'. In the last line *reidun* might be the hero's name. The two preceding lines say 'The best of the sleepless feast – to-day not to be wakened'; that is, he was outstanding at the clamorous feast of Mynyddog, but the next day he was dead.

A.59 = CA. lx

'After wine-feast and mead-feast they went from us, the mail-clad [warriors]; I know the grief for their death. Their slaying came to pass before [they could grow] grey-haired, their host was high-spirited in front of Catraeth. From the retinue of Mynyddog – great sorrow! – but for one man out of three hundred, none came back.'

A.60 = CA. lxi A

This is a close variant of B.20, q.v. 'Set their hands to'; Ifor Williams would now translate 'enjoyed', BBCS. x, 136, but the other still seems preferable.

'After wine-feast and mead-feast they hastened out, men renowned in [battle]-straits, reckless of their lives; in a shining array they fed together round the wine vessel, they set their hands to wine and mead and malt. I have become bitterly sad for the retinue of Mynyddog, I have lost too many of my true kinsmen. Out of three hundred champions who hastened to Catraeth, alas, none came back but for one man.'

A.61 = CA. lxii

For Cadfannan cf. A.3 and 39. If *atre* does mean 'retreat' the line must say that he was always fighting bravely whether the men of Gododdin were advancing or retreating. A word meaning 'deserved' would suit the context better than 'grasped'; possibly a confusion between *talu* 'to pay for, be worth', and *dal* 'to hold' lies behind this.

'In the hosting he used to be always like a ball that bounds (?), and where the retreat (?) was he used to be likewise. The men of Gododdin set their hands to wine and mead, resolute in the straits of hardship on the borderland; and ridden by Cadfannan, there was a red herd of horses, the horseman fierce in the morning.'

A.62 = CA. lxiii A

See note on B.14. 'Sting', see BBCS. XI, 148 f. 'Neddig' is some unknown hero, apparently an ancestor of Merin's.

'The anchor, the scatterer of the men of Deira, the serpent with the terrible sting, he used to trample on dark-blue armour in the forefront of the army; the fearful bear, the violent gate-keeper, he used to trample on spears in the day of battle in the alder-grown moat. A fit successor to Neddig, a lord, truly he brought about through his fury a feast for the birds from the uproarious fight. For your loyal deeds rightly are you called the foremost, the prince, the rampart of warriors. Merin son of Madiain, in a fortunate hour you were born.'

A.63 = CA. lxiv A

This forms a chain with A.64–67; 63, 65, and 66 are variants of the corresponding chain in B.; see the discussion in the note to B.39, and for A.63 see its close variant B.40. The verse begins 'A fitting song of a company was got', and the translation of the rest is identical with B.40.

A.64 = CA. lxv

'A fitting song of a worthy company – uproar, fire, and thunder and spring-tide. The horseman, distinguished for courage in the turmoil, the red reaper, he longed for war; the warrior, eagerly he hastened to battle in whatever land he heard of it, with his shield on his shoulder; he would take up his spear just as if it were sparkling wine from glass vessels. His mead was contained in silver [goblets], but he deserved gold; Gwaednerth son of Llywri was reared on wine.'

A.65 = CA. lxvi A

See the close variant B.39.

'A fitting song of brilliant retinues; and after it has ebbed the river floods. He glutted the grasp of grey eagles' beaks, he made food for carrion birds. Of all the wearers of gold torques who went to Catraeth on the expedition of Mynyddog, the lord of hosts, there came from among the Britons of Gododdin no man without reproach better by far than Cynon.'

A.66 = CA. lxvii A

See the note on B.39.

'A fitting song of a skilful company. A pleasant little place in the world, he was not covetous [of it] (?); what he desired was the acclamation of bards all round the world for [his] gold and great horses and drunkenness on mead; but when he should come from battle, the praise of Cynddilig of Aeron by bloodstained men.'

A.67 = CA. lxviii

The context suggests that 'the daughter of Eudaf' was Mynyddog's wife, and that she played some part in organising the expedition; but Eudaf is unknown. Gwannanon is evidently a region, and compare A.73, where it appears to be on the borders of Gododdin, which would suit here too. It may also occur in B.30, but this is uncertain.

'A fitting song of brilliant retinues, on the expedition of Mynyddog the lord of hosts, and of the daughter of Eudaf the tall who was clothed in purple, the oppressor of Gwanannon, a land of broken men.'

A.68 = CA. lxix A

See the quite close variant B.29 and the discussion on it. 'Their destruction', see BBCS. XXI, 30. 'Were counted up' is the reading of B., which suits better here. On the last sentence see the note on A.2.

'[Even] cowards joined in the praise in the hall, like the fierceness of blazing fire when it has been kindled. On Tuesday they put on their dark-blue armour, on Wednesday their lime-white protective shields were got ready, on Thursday their destruction (?) was certain, on Friday corpses were counted up, on Saturday their united deeds were unrestricted, on Sunday their red blades were plied (?), on Monday streams of blood were seen up to the knees. The men of Gododdin recount that when they came back to Madog's tent after the fatigue [of battle] there returned no more than one man out of a hundred.'

A.69 = CA. lxx A

This is a chain with A.70, and see the respective variants of these two, B.33 and 32. 'In conflict before the boundary of the river-mouth', and, in A.70, 'after the sunset before the border by the river-mouth', is doubtful; the reading of B.33 is probably closest to the original. Anyone tempted to make geographical identifications from 'river-mouth' should bear in mind in any case that the Welsh word means a confluence of two rivers as well as the opening of a river on the sea. Williams' explanation of the word omitted (*twlch*; C.A., p. 279 f.) will not do, since both the Old Irish words he compares are really *tolg*. 'Hawks' = 'warriors'.

'Rising up early in the morn, in conflict before the boundary of the river-mouth, there was a breach, there was a fiery. . . . Like a wild boar you led uphill. He was courteous and tenacious, he was grave, he was a blood-bath of dark-coloured hawks.'

A.70 = CA. lxxi A

See the note on A.69. The second sentence means that to
him, fighting was like a jolly carousal.

> 'Rising up early in the morning, after the sunset before
> the border by the river-mouth, following from outpost
> to outpost, he charged foremost before a hundred men.
> Fiercely you used to make streams of blood, like drink-
> ing mead while laughing; easily (?) you used to strike
> down corpses with a bold swift swordstroke. It was thus
> eagerly he used to slay the enemy, Gwrhafal in the
> army.'

A.71 = CA. lxxii

There are many obscurities in this verse, but apparently
when Ywain was killed his body fell in the river, and he
was unable to fulfil his boasts ('intention'). He used to reward Aneirin for eulogies. 'When a girl' etc. seems to mean
that in matters concerning women he was modest. The
verse begins 'He fell headlong into the depths, the skilful
chief did not hold to his intention; his killing with a
spear (?) was an infraction (?) of privilege. It was Ywain's
custom to mount in the borderland, bending a most excel-
lent spear before lying down (?), pressing hard on the
slaughter; the subject of dirges (?)'. There follow then six
doubtful lines, including a reference to the 'gauntlet which
he carried in his mailcoat-stripping hand'; and it ends
'Modest (?) when a girl was the chief judge, possessor of
horses and dark-blue armour and . . . shields, companion
in conflict, retreating, attacking.'

A.72 = CA. lxxiii

The last sentence seems to mean the hero was cutting his
way through the press to where there was more space for
manoeuvre; cf. Caerwyn Williams in BBCS. XXI, 226.

> 'Leader in slaughter, he led to war; the host of the land

loved the mighty reaper. The green sward [was] bloody around the fresh grave; he had armour over his crimson [garments], a trampler on armour, on armour a trampler. Weariness like death is brought [upon the warriors (?)]; spears in the ribs at the beginning of battle; a path to a clearing (?) was the purpose of his spear-thrust.'

A.73 = CA. lxxiv

The anonymous North Welsh hero of this verse seems to have led a dawn attack on an English palace, ironically called 'a handsome gift' to them (cf. the note on B.34). On Gwanannon see A.67; it appears to be a region on the borders of Gododdin, and since he was presumably killed at Catraeth this seems to imply that Catraeth also was in this borderland. On this see the Appendix no. 1, at the end.

'I sang a famous song about the destruction of your treasure-house and the hall which used to exist. It deserved sweet yellow ensnaring mead, the assault on the warrior's court at dawn; a handsome gift to the hosts of the English, a great penance as long as they may be allowed [to survive]. His glory shall be heard of among the liegemen of Gwynedd, [but] Gwanannon is [his] grave; the steadfast man of Gwynedd, lively in battle, the bull of the army, violent in the conflict of lords before his resting-place in the earth, before lying down [in death]; the borderland of Gododdin is his grave.'

A.74 = CA. lxxv A

See the partial variant B.37. On Pobddelw see the Introduction § 5. The anonymous hero of the verse might be said to have harmed his land by getting killed, along with his men. The next sentence seems to include a picture of a column of spearmen breaking through the enemy, with their spears bristling forwards in precise order.

'[With] an army accustomed to battle, the noble, the

leader of hosts, cruel of hand; he was wise and perfect and proud, he was not acrimonious at the carousal; white (?) [horses] snorted (?) under his protection; he was no profit to the land of Pobddelw. We are called the wing (?) and the van (?) in contest, in the break-through of spears; spears of equal length, the armament of sharpened irons of a champion in . . . , a pike in the din, in the clamour of battle, a man full of vigour with flaming steel against the enemy.'

A.75 = CA. lxxvi

This short verse is obscure, and it is not certain whether any person is named, though there are two words which might be names. The second, *heidyn*, can scarcely be the man who, according to the tradition in the Triads, killed Aneirin (see Introduction § 6), since the hero of this verse must have fallen at Catraeth. It begins 'Battle-horses bore bloodstained battle-harness, a red herd at Catraeth', but the rest, which offers nothing of interest, is not continu-ously clear enough to be worth an attempt at translation.

A.76 = CA. lxxvii

This again seems anonymous. Williams, it is true, takes the word translated here as 'the courteous one' (*mynawc*) as a name (CA., p. 298), but such a name appears unknown, and it is more likely to be the adjective, as in the next line. To emend to *Mynydawc* will scarcely do, since the evidence that he went to Catraeth and was killed there is wholly negative, and it is incredible that this would be the case if it were true. The verse must surely be in praise of the one who escaped, probably Cynon son of Clydno of Eidyn, and the second sentence seems to refer to some previous fight near Edinburgh. 'He set up a stronghold' means he drew up his men in a square like a fortress of shields; 'because he feasted', i.e. he took part in the feast and the conse-quent expedition.

'Of the courteous one of Gododdin it shall be told forth; courteous in the share-out, he shall be lamented. With the fury of flame, he did not retreat in front of Eidyn, he stationed his true men in the van, he set up a stronghold in the face of battle, fiercely he attacked the bold [enemy]; because he feasted he suffered great hardship. Of the retinue of Mynyddog there did not escape but one man, brandishing his weapon, huge.'

A.77 = CA. lxxviii

'Since the loss of Moried there has been no shield. They supported and extolled the lone champion; he was accustomed to carry blue blades in his hand, heavy javelins – they endangered (?) the chief endangerer (?) – on a dapple-grey arching-necked steed. The fallen in battle [were] cut down before his blades; when he conquered in his fight he was no deserter. He deserved praise [and] sweet ensnaring mead.'

A.78 = CA. lxxix A

A close variant of B. 1, q.v. 'Had arisen' (*ry godessyn*) is the reading of B., and is probably correct; the *ry gollessyn*, 'had been lost', of A. is less likely to be right and is rejected here.

'I saw an array, they came from the headland, and splendidly they attacked around the conflagration. I saw the accustomed muster hastening to the town, and the men of the grandson of Nwython had arisen. I saw men in array, they came at the battle-shout; and the head of Dyfnwal Frych, ravens gnawed it.'

A.79 = CA. lxxx

For Cynddilig compare A.66. 'The enemy from overseas' must imply that it was remembered the English were from the Continent. 'It was his custom' etc. suggests that he led a troop of ten, counting himself.

'Good, triumphant, light-hearted, fair, the backbone of a timid host; with his blue [sword] a cause of retreat to the enemy from overseas; manly and mighty, of massive hand, with courageous heart, skilful (?) – they charged upon him. It was his custom to attack in front of nine champions in the presence of the battle-shout of the army, and to provoke them. I love the victorious one; he sat on the couch; Cynddilig of Aeron, the eloquent, the lion.'

A.80 = CA. lxxxi

On the son of Ceidio see the Introduction § 5. 'To find fault with the spear', that is, not to have been so pugnacious. It is uncertain whether *uffin* is a place-name.

'I should have liked to attack at Catraeth among the foremost in return for mead in the hall and drink of wine. I should have liked him to find fault with the spear before he was killed, [far (?)] from his green Uffin (?); I should have loved the man of famous race who endured bloody slaughter. He struck with his sword in the fierce fight. The [roll of] valour does not tell, in the presence of the men of Gododdin, that the famous son of Ceidio was not surpassing in battle.'

A.81 = CA. lxxxii

For the names mentioned in this verse see A.31–33. 'Of most valiant station', i.e. they took up posts of danger in fight.

'It is grief to me that after the toil [of battle] they suffered the agony of death in affliction, and a second heavy grief it is to me to have seen our men falling headlong; and it is continual moaning and sorrow after the fiery men in the clodded earth – Rhufon and Gwgon, Gwion and Gwlyged, men of most valiant station, strong in strife. After the battle may their souls get welcome in the land of Heaven, the dwelling of plenty.'

A.82 = CA. lxxxiii

'His advice' etc., i.e., in the council-chamber; 'was waited for', or, 'prevailed' or 'prospered', see Williams in Cymm. Trans., 1940, p. 82. The last word in the verse is obscure.

'He drove back the conflict through a pool of blood, like a brave man he slew the rank which did not flee; Tafloew would toss off a glass of mead in style (?), and in the presence of princes he would overthrow an army. His advice was waited for (?) where the many did not speak, and if it had been cruel it would not have been allowed. Before the charge of axe strokes and long sharpened swords there arose a noisy feast. . . .'

A.83 = CA. lxxxiv

'A privileged position' means a post of honour, in the van. Apparently Tyngyr was killed in an unsuccessful cavalry charge.

'The haven of the army, the harbour of the spear (?), with a supreme host in a privileged position in conflict on the day of battle; they were bold, after drunkenness and mead-drinking. There was no help against our success (?) on the day of the mighty charge, when it was told that an assault of men and horses was broken – Tyngyr's doom!'

A.84 = CA. lxxxv

There are various difficulties in this verse. Argoed (lit. 'In Front of the Forest') is a name which occurs in various parts of the Brittonic world, including Brittany, but in this case it is very likely the unidentified Argoed Llwyfain of the Taliesin eulogies on Urien, somewhere in Rheged. 'Disposing the banquet' etc. suggests that Geraint was a sort of Master of Ceremonies in Mynyddog's hall. 'Reclining', reading *gosgoyw* with G., sv. 'The men of the South'; putting this together with the fact that Geraint was the name of one traditional and one historical king of Devon (neither

contemporaries of Catraeth), Williams suggests that this
one too was from there (CA., p. 314). But on this, see A.27;
and there is no real reason at all to suppose he was not from
northern England, quite possibly Rheged, as just suggested.

'When there comes upon me a host of anxieties . . . ,
[my] breath fails (?) as if with strenuous running, and
straightway I weep. I would grieve for my dear one, the
dear one whom I had loved, the glorious stag. Alas for
him who was wont to draw himself up with the men of
Argoed. For the profit of kings, well did he attack the
hosts of the country, the bristling wood [of spears], the
grievous flood [of the enemy], in return for the banquets.
Disposing the banquet, he led us up to the bright fire
and to the reclining (?) [seat covered with] white fleece.
Geraint – his battle-cry was raised in front of the men
of the South; flashing and bright was the white appearance of his shield; the lord of the spear, the generous
renowned lord, courteous, [in liberality like] the sea (?)
– I know his nature. I know [you] generous Geraint,
you were noble.'

A.85 = CA. lxxxvi

'His fame, his glory, is unrestrained, the strong anchor in
the conflict, the mighty eagle among wrathful men.
Steadfast in battle, Eiddef was handsome, he led the
horses, very swift in fight, fostered with wine from the
cup. Before his green grave [was dug] and his cheeks
grew pale, he was a banqueter over the cup of fine
mead.'

A.86 = CA. lxxxvii A

This is a variant of B.4; see the discussion in the note on
that verse. It is very close to B.4, so close that there is no
need to give a separate translation (bearing in mind the
differences in the forms of the names mentioned above),
except as follows: For B.'s 'his battle-horses and his blood-

stained armour were seen around the Aled' A. has 'they were called on around the Aled in the battle of horses and bloodstained armour;' for the partly rather unclear passage which follows in B., A. gives a less obscure variant, 'an unshaken army, they are mighty in battle, the gravel of the enclosure is red when they have been provoked'; for B.'s 'son of a rightful king, lord of the men of Gwynedd' A. has 'son of a rightful lord among the men of Gwynedd'; and for B.'s 'before the cheek of the generous, thoughtful, sage man was buried in the earth his fame brought visiting throngs' A. has 'before the cheek of the liberal, generous, thoughtful, undaunted man of glory and gifts was buried in the earth, it is sad that Garthwys', etc. On 'the gravel of the enclosure is red' see § 9 above.

A.87 = CA. lxxxviii

This is the famous interpolated cradle-song; see the Introduction § 14. 'Phew, phew'; the mother whistles to the child, and sings to him (this must be the meaning of *gochan-*, cf. the Old Irish cognate *fo-cain*, 'sings to').

'Dinogad's coat is of many colours, many colours. I made it of the skins of martens. Phew, phew, a whistling! Let us sing to him, the eight slaves sing to him. When your father would go to hunt, with a spear-shaft on his shoulder and a club in his hand, he called to the nimble (?) hounds, 'Giff, Gaff, seize, seize, fetch, fetch!' He killed fish in his coracle as when a lion kills a . . . When your father went to the mountain he would bring back a roebuck, a wild pig, a stag, a speckled grouse from the mountain, a fish from the falls of Derwennydd. Out of all those that your father got at with his dart, whether wild pig or fox or . . . , none escaped unless it had wings.'

A.88 = CA. lxxxix

At the end of this verse the scribe A. broke off his copy of

the *Gododdin* near the top of page 23 of the MS. The name
Penclwyd is unidentified.

'Bereavement has come upon me unsought; there comes
not, there will not come to me any that may be more
grievous. None was reared in a hall who would be
bolder than he, nor more steadfast in battle; and at the
ford of Penclwyd his horses were in the forefront; his
fame was spread afar, his lime-white shield was broken;
and before Gwair the tall was buried under the sod he
deserved his horns of mead, the one son of Fferfarch.'

THE GORCHANAU

On these see the Introduction § 15. The hand A. began writing them at the top of p. 25 of the MS.

The Gorchan of Tudfwlch; CA., p. 50.

On Tudfwlch see the Introduction § 8. The disjointed style, in addition to the usual other puzzles, makes it particularly difficult to piece the fragments together into a coherent picture, but the first few lines begin with a battle scene and appear to go on to a carousal in the hall afterwards ('the bitter alder-wood cup' probably refers to a wooden bowl full of some bitter drink like bragget); therefore not the feast before Catraeth but some previous one celebrating a fight in which Tudfwlch had distinguished himself? The *gorchan* is made up of long-lines rhyming together, the rhyme changing every few long-lines; but there are no separate verses.

The poem is headed with a rubric, and the text then takes up, starting with a phrase which found its way into A.23 (see the note on that verse).

'Here begins the Gorchan of Tudfwlch.
When the weapons were scattered and the ranks broken, [after] the uproar in the massacre, in the presence of riches, in the presence of magnificence, in the presence of splendour [and of] the bitter alder-wood cup as well as the spiral drinking-horns and the curved swords, as long as I saw him he was praised – the lone champion of the retinues, pale-faced, matchless. . . .'

Much of the above is doubtful, and what follows is still more so, but there seems to be a reference to vegetation growing over 'his' grave (no hero is yet named), and to fame etc. passing away; 'and Eifionydd lamented the [death-]day of the man of bright glory', and there were 'loud thunderous [cries] around Tal Hen Ban' (on these places, and Tudfwlch's connections with them, see the Introduction, § 8). The poet continues:

'. . . Like a wolf at his food, he was a wolf at the ford in his prime; with eyes like spears, shining like a snake's from a snakes' lair. You are mighty, a net for the mighty, beloved of girls; you loved a life of danger, I should have loved you to be alive, rampart of valour, martial bull. I mourn your death; you loved discord, you with the fury of the sea in the front ranks of the men of war. . . .'

In this, 'like a wolf at his food' etc. hardly means he wolfed his food, but rather that he attacked the enemy at the strategic point on the ford like a wolf attacking its food. There follow some obscure phrases containing unidentified place-names, and it continues:

'. . . To the profit of the infantry, he drove back four hosts for the sake of the country, four armies of the armies of the world; with his shield split and his blade in the hair [of the enemy, and] four-sided (?) shields. A man frenzied (?) with pale horns of mead in the morning, a man of lawful titles, dressed in purple, the haven of the army, Tudfwlch's arms [wielded weapons (?)] with bitter fury . . . In return for mead and ale the company went across their . . . boundary. Active among the spears, he was worthy (?) in upholding the law. Cynan and Cynon and Teithfyw from Anglesey, like [men with] overwhelming numbers; Tudfwlch and Cyfwlch who made breaches in the summits of strongholds, in the company of Mynyddog their drinks were bitter. A year of mourning is mine for the men of Catraeth who fostered me; for their steel blades and their pure mead from drinking-horns. When the weapons were scattered and the ranks broken, I heard the uproar.   And so it ends.'

The Gorchan of Adebon; CA., p. 52

On this, see the Introduction § 15. Adebon is quite unknown elsewhere. The poem has no connection whatever with Catraeth or even with heroic poetry (towards the end there are one or two obscure references to fighting, but it is not clear that these are not simply proverbs like the rest), and it will not be discussed here.

The Gorchan of Cynfelyn; CA., p. 53

This lay is even more obscure than that of Tudfwlch. Nothing is known about Cynfelyn except what the poem tells, that he was son of Tegfan son of Cadfan and came from North Wales. It opens as follows:

'Here now begins the Gorchan of Cynfelyn.

If I were to compose poetry, if I were to sing . . .' etc. It then goes on to a very unclear comparison with the story of Twrch Trwyth, the magic boar hunted by King Arthur in the Mabinogion story of *Culhwch and Olwen*,[1] which is particularly important because it bears witness to the existence of this tale very early (assuming that it is not an interpolation here), earlier than the otherwise oldest known reference to it in Nennius's *Historia Brittonum*, c. 73, early ninth century. The hero is described as attacking in a river (as Twrch Trwyth fought Arthur's men in the Severn, but this comparison is apparently not explicitly made), and at what seem to be a number of unidentified places. 'A due slaying of the Angles' is mentioned, the only place in the manuscript where this name occurs. The hero strikes shields 'through stud, through rivet' etc., as described in the Introduction § 9. A slightly less obscure passage follows; Gwynasedd is known elsewhere as a woman's name but appears to be a man here, killed by Cynfelyn:

[1] See the translation by G. Jones and T. Jones, *The Mabinogion* (London; Everyman no. 97: 1949), pp. 95 ff.

'. . . And a deep distress comes upon Gwynasedd the yellow-haired, his blood all over him; the sparkles of fine yellow mead are no more seen; his blood all over him before the battalions of Cynfelyn, Cynfelyn the furious, the bold, the foremost with his spear, who fed birds on bloody corpses. Long-striding [horses] galloped with the thighs of the generous [warriors] upon them, as swift as the speed of madmen running over grassy land (?). The lord, the enricher of his country, it is mine to bewail him until I reach my silent [death-]day; the feller of the enemy with his broad-hafted weapon. The Gorchan of Cynfelyn is the glory of honoured songs; the Gorchan of Cynfelyn who guarded the borderland, a sagacious man of war, Gwynedd was his land. . . .'

A short passage even more difficult follows, including a reference to *Eidyn gaer*, 'the fortified town Eidyn', and to 'the horses of Eithinyn' (who appears in the *Gododdin* in B.30 and 31 and A.37, 38, and 53). It then goes on:

'. . . The Gorchan of Cynfelyn appended to the *Gododdin*, it has made ample approbation of the man. He gave me his fine gilded spear, may it be for the good of his soul; the son of Tegfan is honoured according to the multitude of his gifts, the grandson of Cadfan, the pillar of fury.[1] When weapons were hurled over the battle-wolves[2] . . . on the day of stress. Three men and three score and three hundred went to the land (?)[3] of Catraeth; of those that hastened forth after the mead [from the hands] of servants, none came back but three[4] – Cynon and Cadraith and Cadlew of Cadnant, and I after my bloody fall, the true son of prophecy;[5] they ransomed me with pure gold and steel and silver; harm

[1] That is, the upholder, the rallying-point, in battle.
[2] A clear reference to the use of javelins.   [3] Or 'battle'.
[4] See the Introduction § 7.
[5] On *mab coel*, and the story of Aneirin's 'ransom', see the Introduction § 6.

have they got, not defence. The Gorchan of the battle-troops of Cynfelyn.

Here ends the Gorchan of Cynfelyn.'

There follows then the rubric discussed in the Introduction § 15, q.v.

The Gorchan of Maeldderw; CA., p. 55

This is by far the most obscure section in all the Book of Aneirin, and it was in connection with it that Sir Ifor Williams gave the despairing cry mentioned above in the Preface. Maeldderw is not known elsewhere, and we gather very little about him from his *gorchan*, except that he seems to be called at one point 'lord of the northern region'. The title of the poem is given as part of the above-mentioned rubric: 'Here now begins the Gorchan of Maeldderw. Taliesin sang it, and gave to it as high a rank as to all the verses of the *Gododdin* and its three *gorchanau* in the poetic competition.'

The lay itself appears to commence 'The meanders of two river-mouths round the city. I am kept awake for the lime-white shield, for the bright one, the roving cruel one, breaching the battle, famous, seeking out conflict, with his chequered clothes all bloodstained, tattered and red, with young warriors whose charge was irresistible'. The 'city' (fortified town) is unknown, but at any rate clearly not Edinburgh. 'I am kept awake for' is a bardic expression for 'I mourn'. 'Lime-white shield' (*calch*), i.e. Maeldderw the protector; considering the common use of *calch* in this sense, this seems preferable to 'the white one'. After some puzzling phrases, the hero seems to be called 'a man who hastened when the alarm was raised, a bedfellow of the beer-hall', on which last phrase see the Introduction § 10. Further on he is called 'the outer gate of the stronghold of

Eidyn (*esgor Eidin*)', but for the rest, though some phrases can be made out (Williams' 'ray of uncertain light here and there') it is not worth attempting a translation, as nothing of much interest is revealed, though one may note that near the end there seems to be a reference to 'a claim to the splendour of the Lord above', and the phrase 'at the end may he attain the Land above'.

Concordance of CA. With the Rendering in Part II

i = A.1
ii = A.2
iii = A.3
iv = A.4
v = A.5
vi = A.6
vii = A.7
viii = A.8
ix = A.9
x = A.10
xi = A.11
xii = A.12
xiii = A.13
xiv = A.14
xv = A.15
xvi = A.16
xvii = A.17
xviii = A.18
xix = A.19
xx A = A.20
xx B = B.12
xxi = A.21
xxii A = A.22
xxii B = B.13
xxiii A = A.23
xxiii B = B.11
xxiv = A.24
xxv = A.25
xxvi A = A.26
xxvi B = B.18
xxvii = A.27
xxviii = A.28
xxix = A.29
xxx = A.30
xxxi = A.31
xxxii = A.32
xxxiii = A.33
xxxiv = A.34
xxxv = A.35
xxxvi = A.36
xxxvii = A.57
xxxviii = A.37
xxxix A = A.38
xxxix B = A.53

xl = B.30
xli = B.31
xlii = A.39
xliii A = A.40
xliii B = B.5
xliv A = A.41
xliv B = B.6
xlv A = A.42
xlv B = B.25
xlv C = B.35
xlvi = A.43
xlvii = A.44
xlviii = A.45
xlix = A.46
l = A.47
li A = A.48
li B = B.24
li C = B.3
lii = A.49
liii = A.50
liv A = A.51
liv B = B.7
lv A = A.52
lv B = B.2
lvi = A.54
lvii = A.55
lviii = A.56
lix = A.58
lx = A.59
lxi A = A.60
lxi B = B.20
lxii = A.61
lxiii A = A.62
lxiii B = B.15
lxiii C = B.16
lxiii D = B.14
lxiii E = B.36
lxiv A = A.63
lxiv B = B.40
lxv = A.64
lxvi A = A.65
lxvi B = B.39
lxvii A = A.66

lxvii B = B.42
lxviii = A.67
lxix A = A.68
lxix B = B.29
lxx A = A.69
lxx B = B.33
lxxi A = A.70
lxxi B = B.32
lxxii = A.71
lxxiii = A.72
lxxiv = A.73
lxxv A = A.74
lxxv B = B.37
lxxvi = A.75
lxxvii = A.76
lxxviii = A.77
lxxix A = A.78
lxxix B = B.1
lxxx = A.79
lxxxi = A.80
lxxxii = A.81
lxxxiii = A.82
lxxxiv = A.83
lxxxv = A.84
lxxxvi = A.85
lxxxvii A = A.86
lxxxvii B = B.4
lxxxviii = A.87
lxxxix = A.88
xc = B.8
xci = B.9
xcii = B.10
xciii = B.17
xciv = B.19
xcv = B.21
xcvi = B.22
xcvii = B.23
xcviii = B.26
xcix = B.27
c = B.28
ci = B.34
cii = B.38
ciii = B.41

Index

Welsh
  contingent, 7, 27-8
  genealogies, 20, 28, 71
  heroic literature, 64
  Old, 43
  phonology of early, 55-6, 86-7,
    89-90
  poetry, 9, 31, 44, 133
  saga (legend, narrative
    tradition), 9, 11, 20, 21-2,
    23
Wid, 130
widows, 102, 126, 139
Williams, Caerwyn, 128, 144
Williams, Sir Ifor, 3, 14, 16,
    21 n, 23, 24 n, 25, 42, 43,
    47 n, 55, 59, 61, 62 n, 66,
    69, 71, 75, 75 n, 77, 78,
    79, 80, 83, 86, 88, 91, 95,
    97, 98, 134, 135, 140, 143,
    146, 149, 150, 157
wine
  distributing, 127-8
  drinking, 35, 36, 102, 106,
    107, 109, 110, 122, 123,
    124, 125, 140, 141, 142
  earning, 36, 103, 117, 132,
    148
  feast, 127, 130, 139, 140

wine—*contd.*
  vessels, 35, 102, 106, 117,
    140, 142, 150
wings, the, 30, 101, 112, 137,
    139, 146
wolves
  as carrion beasts, 41, 117, 129
  heroes compared to, 41, 104,
    111, 154, 156
  tackling, with bare hands,
    101, 133
Wotadini (Otadinoi, Votadini),
    5, 69, 70, 74, 75, 81
wyvern, 127

York, 61
Yorkshire, 6, 7, 8, 81
Young, P., 16 n
Ysgyrran, father of Gwefrfawr,
    117
Ywain (unidentified), 144
Ywain, son of Beli, king of
    Strathclyde, 48, 132
Ywain Cyfeiliog, 53
Ywain, son of Eulad, 129
Ywain Gwynedd, 53
Ywain, son of Hywel Dda, 65
Ywain, son of Marro, 115
Ywain, son of Urien, 26 n